Coffee at Luke's

D1510081

OTHER TITLES IN THE SMART POP SERIES

Coffee at Luke's

An Unauthorized
Gilmore Girls *Gabfest*

EDITED BY

Jennifer Crusie

WITH Leah Wilson

BENBELLA BOOKS, INC.
Dallas, Texas

BOCA RATON PUBLIC LIBRARY
BOCA RATON, FLORIDA

THIS PUBLICATION HAS NOT BEEN PREPARED, APPROVED, OR LICENSED BY ANY ENTITY THAT CREATED OR PRODUCED THE WELL-KNOWN TELEVISION SERIES *GILMORE GIRLS*.

"Whimsy Goes with Everything" © 2006 by Heather Swain
"Boys Not Allowed" © 2006 by Jennifer Armstrong
"When Paris Met Rory" © 2006 by Stephanie Whiteside
"Mothers, Daughters, and Gilmore Girls" © 2006 by Janine Hiddlestone
"The Best-Friend Mom" © 2006 by Stephanie Lehmann
"In Defense of Emily Gilmore" © 2006 by Charlotte Fullerton
"My Three Dads" © 2006 by Miellyn Fitzwater
"Your Guide to the Real Stars Hollow Business World" © 2006 by Sara Morrison
"Happiness Under Glass: The Truth about Lorelai and Life in Stars Hollow"
    © 2006 by Jill Winters
"It's Not Luke's Stubble" © 2006 by Stephanie Rowe
"Dining with the Gilmores" © 2006 by Gregory Stevenson
"Reading, Rory, and Relationships" © 2006 by Maryelizabeth Hart
"'That's What You Get, Folks, For Makin' Whoopee'" © 2006 by Kristen Kidder
"Golden Age *Gilmore Girls*: How Classic Hollywood Comedy Defines the Show"
    © 2006 by Chris McCubbin
"'Mama Don't Preach': Class, Culture, and Lorelai Gilmore as Bizarro-World Suffragette"
    © 2006 by Carol Cooper
"*Coffee at Luke's*-isms" © 2007 by BenBella Books, Inc.
Additional Materials © 2007 by Jennifer Crusie

All rights reserved. No part of this book may be used or reproduced in any manner whatsoever without written permission except in the case of brief quotations embodied in critical articles or reviews.

 BenBella Books, Inc.
6440 N. Central Expressway, Suite 617
Dallas, TX 75206
www.benbellabooks.com
Send feedback to feedback@benbellabooks.com

Printed in the United States of America
10 9 8 7 6 5 4 3 2 1

Library of Congress Cataloging-in-Publication Data

Coffee at Luke's : an unauthorized Gilmore Girls gabfest / edited by Jennifer Crusie with Leah Wilson.
    p. cm.
    ISBN 1-933771-17-8
    1. Gilmore girls (Television program) I. Crusie, Jennifer. II. Wilson, Leah.

    PN1992.77.G54C64 2007
    791.45'72—dc22
                                                                            2007006643

Proofreading by Megan Stolz, Anjali Lahiri, and Jennifer Thomason
Cover design by Allison Bard
Text design and composition by John Reinhardt Book Design
Printed by Bang Printing

Distributed by Independent Publishers Group
To order call (800) 888-4741 • www.ipgbook.com

For special sales contact Yara Abuata at yara@benbellabooks.com

Contents

Second Hamlet to the Right: Stars Hollow

The Best Things in Life: Food, Books, and Sex

There's Reality and Then There's Lorelai: Gilmore Girls and the Real World

Introduction

Speaking of
the Gilmore Girls...

WELCOME TO *COFFEE AT LUKE'S*, a collection of people talking about *Gilmore Girls*, which is *so* appropriate. The success of *Gilmore Girls* can be attributed to many things: the beauty and charm of its protagonists, Lorelai the mother we all wish we'd had (or been), and Rory the daughter we all wish we'd been (or had); the warm and quirky charm of Stars Hollow, the community where nobody is ever lost or alone; the slow-burn sizzle of the romance between Lorelai and Luke, now gone horribly awry but still a winner for six long seasons; the parade of Rory's boyfriends, each more attractive and impossible than the last; the anyone-can-relate Friday night disasters of dinner with Emily and Richard; and the crackle of the supporting cast, especially the acerbic Paris (who takes antisocial disorder to new heights), Kirk (who makes cluelessness an art form), and Miss Patty (who embraces life to the point of smothering it in her bosom). Even Paul Anka the dog has his own dysfunctional charm. Yes, all of these aspects contribute to making *Gilmore Girls* a TiVo staple, but the real draw that's kept viewers coming back season after season? Oh, that's the talk.

Yep, it's the whip-fast, quip-smart, sassy patter that Lorelai dishes out and Rory bats back like some kind of party game for smarty pants, the Cool Girls verbal Twister, pitched right at us so we all can play. All teleplays have dialogue but very few of them use it well, and none of them rely on it the way that *Gilmore Girls* does: almost to the point of being a talking heads show, with very little physical comedy

1

and fairy tale sets that function as a backdrop for beautiful people adept at delivering complex speech at the speed of light. Crafting that speech is a tightrope act the writers walk every week, and they walk it pretty damn well, in part, I think, because they keep in mind the basic rules for great dialogue:

Keep it moving.

Boy, do they. Well, they have to. On a typical television show, one page of script equals one minute of show and the average television script is about fifty to fifty-five pages (leaving room to cut the filmed results to forty-eight minutes of running time), but the *Gilmore Girls* scripts run seventy-seven to seventy-eight pages. That means no dawdling, so the characters rattle off the line like escapees from *His Girl Friday*. Call it *Our Girls Tuesday*, the screwball fastball of comic repartee that's not only swift but complex, often overlapping not only conversations but also conflicts:

> RORY: Hey. My mom's not wearing any underwear.
> LORELAI: Oh!
> RORY: Well you aren't.
> TAYLOR: You're just being selfish, Luke.
> LORELAI: Still they don't notice. I can't take it anymore.
> TAYLOR: We're talking about the spirit of fall.
> LORELAI: (gets the coffee herself and lifts the cover off the muffins) What kind of muffin do you want?
> RORY: Blueberry.
> LUKE: You know where you can stick the spirit of fall? (hands Lorelai a utensil to pick up the muffins) Here, don't use your hands.
> TAYLOR: I don't think you're taking me seriously.
> LUKE: What gave you that idea? (to Lorelai, who is leaving) No tip?
> LORELAI: Oh, yeah, here's a tip…serve your customers.
> LUKE: Here's another…don't sit on any cold benches. ("Kiss and Tell," 1-7)

It takes very good writers to put dialogue like that on the page and keep it not only clear but entertaining while moving the story along. If you took the character tags off those lines and read it, you'd still know what show it came from because dialogue like that only happens in Stars Hollow.

Give everybody the best lines.

How can the writers do that? When characters are so distinct that they can't possibly talk alike, the best lines for them can only be theirs. There are several television writers who are well-known for their dialogue, but too many of them fall into the trap of everybody-sounds-the-same. This rarely happens on *Gilmore Girls* where you can pretty much tell without tags who says, "This festival is commemorating the founding of our town, young lady" ("Star-Crossed Lovers and Other Strangers," 1-16). Or who says, "You know, it's times like these that you realize what is truly important in your life. I'm so glad I had all that sex" ("Say Goodnight, Gracie," 3-20). Or who says, "Look, I've had my peace with the fact that everyone who calls here is a notch above brain dead, and that the pennies I am thrown each week are in exchange for me dealing with these people in a nonviolent manner, and usually that is fine, but today, sorry lady, I have ennui" ("Love, Daisies, and Troubadours," 1-21). Or, God help him, who says, "Well, ladies and gentlemen, much like the Israelites of Yore, the Stars Hollow Minutemen languished in the desert for forty years. But tonight, there was no Promised Land, no New Canaan, only a humiliating five to one defeat at the merciless hands of the West Hartford Wildcats. So it's back to the desert for the Minutemen, perhaps for another forty years. Of course, by then, I'll be seventy years old. A lot of the rest of you will probably be dead. Taylor, you'll be dead. Babette, Miss Patty...that man there in the hat" ("Face-Off," 3-15). Even the walk-on parts are worth listening to because even they have places they've been and places they're going to, full and fascinating lives, pieces of which they let drop into the story like seasoning. Everybody gets the best lines.

Talk up to your viewer.

I don't know when "dumbing down" began to seem like a good idea on TV, but it's a mistake and the writers on *Gilmore Girls* know it.

Their mantra is "Everybody's smart and so are you." So what if some of the allusions go over some viewers' heads? The rest of them won't. I know this because I'm a complete music illiterate, but I never feel lost when Rory and Lane talk about groups or CDs. That takes some very careful writing and I'm appreciative. It's conversation where everybody knows the game, and you feel as though you could play, too, if only you were there. But what's really impressive is the breadth: allusions to film, television, literature, music, society, and politics, spanning decades, are just dropped into the conversation and then trampled on as the characters rush on to the next crisis, never slowing to complain or explain:

> LORELAI (to Rory): We're not gonna have this fight in a flowery bedroom with dentists singing "Gypsies, Tramps and Thieves" in the background. It's too David Lynch! ("The Road Trip to Harvard," 2-4)

> PARIS: Wow, you're always so Desmond Tutu-y. This is refreshing. ("We've Got Magic To Do," 6-5)

> BABETTE: Now don't you freak out. Morey hates being the first anywhere. He thinks it hurts his street credibility.
> MOREY: Charlie Parker was late to everything.
> BABETTE: Charlie Parker had more drugs in him than a Rite-Aid. Forget Charlie Parker. ("The Bracebridge Dinner," 2-10)

> LORELAI: You will say nothing, you will do nothing, you will sit in the corner and offer no opinions and pull a full-on Clarence Thomas. ("Secrets and Loans," 2-11)

> EMILY: What do you think of the Romanovs?
> LUKE: They probably had it coming. ("Dead Uncles and Vegetables," 2-17)

And my personal favorite:

> LUKE: Very romantic.
> LORELAI: Says the man who yelled "Finally!" at the end of *Love Story*. ("Let the Games Begin," 3-8)

Dumb dialogue is boring dialogue; the writers on *Gilmore Girls* never make that mistake.

Remember that the best dialogue is the stuff you can't hear.

I'm a dialogue junkie in my own work, so believe me when I tell you that the most important thing about dialogue is what isn't said. On-the-nose talk is another form of dumbing down, leaving the viewer no chance to make the connections; worse than that, it's not real. People in real life do not tell it like is, they tell it slant, and that's why the good stuff isn't in the words, it's all around them.

It's in the spaces between the beautifully parallel non-sequiturs, like this exchange of afflictions:

MADELINE: My brother has measles.
LOUISE: My mom's having an affair. ("Concert Interruptus," 1-13)

It's in the rhythms of the you-know-damn-well-what-I-mean rapid fire exchanges that read like poetry:

LORELAI: She's not going on your motorcycle.
DEAN: I don't have a motorcycle.
LORELAI: She's not going on your motorcycle.
DEAN: Fine, she won't go on my motorcycle. ("Kiss and Tell," 1-7)

It's in the exasperated missed connections that make conversations look like performances by trapeze artists with sweaty hands:

EMILY: So what exactly is going on between the two of you?
LUKE: Nothing. Really. We're friends, that's it.
EMILY: You're idiots, the both of you. ("Forgiveness and Stuff," 1-10)

And it's the dialogue that plays on the viewer's knowledge of the world of the show, written with haiku-like economy:

LORELAI: The world changes when it snows. It's quiet. Everything softens.
MICHEL: It's your mother.
LORELAI: And then the rain comes. ("Love and War and Snow," 1-8)

It takes a great deal of trust in and respect for your audience to leave the best part unsaid, and the writers of *Gilmore Girls* clearly have a lot of both; it's not that surprising, then, that viewers have repaid them with the same.

Given that it's such a showcase of dialogue, it's not surprising that *Gilmore Girls* is one of the most quoted series in the history of TV or that, when I read the essays for this collection, so many of them cited such terrific exchanges from past seasons. They were having so much fun, I wanted to play, too, so I went back and found quotes that evoked the spirit of their essays, recalling how the people of Stars Hollow spoke about personal relationships (they're terrible at them), parenting (still trying to get it right), the town (quirky doesn't begin to describe it), the good things in life (food, books, and sex, not necessarily in that order), and reality (always optional). The opinions here are many and varied but the essayists all share a love of the show and the fast-talking people in and behind it, and they're all here to, well, talk about it. Because in the world of *Gilmore Girls*, that's what you do. . . .

> RORY: Well, you know, I guess we don't have to talk about...stuff. Yeah...
> LORELAI: Who say we always have to be talking? We can not talk!
> RORY: Of course we can.
> (The two pause for a moment.)
> LORELAI: Okay, we should probably talk about how we're not gonna talk...("The Long Morrow," 7-1)

So welcome to the *Gilmore Girls* anthology. I hope you find something terrific on every page. And when you're done, I'll be at Luke's if you want to, you know, discuss it.

Talk to you soon,

Jenny

It All Comes Out in Moron: Personal Relationships

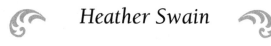

Heather Swain

Whimsy Goes with Everything

KIRK: Well, first I read the sign and then I tried the door in case it was some sort of elaborate ruse.
LORELAI: Designed to keep only you out?
KIRK: There's precedent. ("Help Wanted," 2-20)

There are those who feel that the population of Stars Hollow is a little eccentric, but Heather Swain understands them all, every one of them, including Kirk. *Especially* Kirk.

I'VE DECIDED TO MOVE to Stars Hollow. I've had enough of New York City with all its hubbub and rigmarole. Who needs fifty-nine dollar, truffle-topped, wagyu beef burgers? Who wants to wait six months for a table at one of Mario Battali's forty-seven new Italian restaurants? I certainly never need to see Hugh Jackman run around Broadway in a white leisure suit again. Or stand beside the next Bernard Goetz on my morning subway commute. It's enough to drive a sane person completely *Taxi Driver*. I don't want to wake up one day, shave my head into a Mohawk, and start yelling "You talking to me?" in the mirror. What I need is a nice, quiet little town, full of fine folks, where I can be me. Besides, there's someone in Stars Hollow I find quite enchanting.

Anyway, what's New York got that Stars Hollow can't offer? Restaurants? What about Luke's? Now that's a damn fine diner with good coffee, and I hear the meatloaf is excellent. Bakeries? Weston's has twenty-seven kinds of pie and thirty-four flavors of ice cream. Mincemeat with praline pecan? Shoofly with butter brickle? You could probably get it there. And the gourmet market, Doose's, sells everything from Easy Mac to aged Camembert. (Although, personally I prefer a nice soy

9

cheese, what with my lactose intolerance and all.) Plus entertainment! You wouldn't believe the festivals, parades, celebrations, and cultural events such a little burg puts on. I'll take the Stars Hollow Firelight Festival over Shakespeare in Central Park any day, because what's more romantic, celebrating two star-crossed lovers drawn together by random astrological events or watching Meryl Streep and Christopher Walken belt out show tunes in the musical adaptation of Bertolt Brecht's *Mother Courage and Her Children*? I think we all know the answer.

Won't I miss all the characters—the loudmouths, eccentrics, artists, and nut jobs—in New York City, you might want to ask. The Julian Schnabels, the Bella Abzugs, the Koches, the Clintons, the Hiltons, the Trumps. The buskers, the beggars, and those guys in wheelchairs who sell funny little knit finger puppets outside subway stations. That's what gives the city its edge. Its panache. Its vroom, vroom, hum-min-na, hum-min-na! Well, let me tell you, if there is one thing Stars Hollow has, it's character, baby, pure character. Character is what makes that town work, and there's one character in particular who keeps me coming back for more.

Sure, sure, things happen in Stars Hollow. People date. Fall in love. Fall out of love. Plan weddings, get married, or skip out on weddings. Go to college, drop out of college, go back to college. Get sick, get well, get over it, get arrested. Have fights, make up. Start businesses, start families, start fires. The usual things that make up life happen there, but those kinds of things happen wherever you go—Beverly Hills, Capeside Mass., the O.C. It's the people those things happen to that make it all the more interesting in Stars Hollow. That's why I'm moving there. I think I could fit in. Make friends. Become a part of the community. Maybe even fall in love with someone special. You know who I'm talking about, don't you? Because, admit it. You feel it, too. I'm blushing. Seriously. It's Kirk.

Kirk Gleason: entrepreneur, artiste, town docent. I love him. But not in the way that you might think. I'm not talking in the pedestrian, over-used trite way that the word *love* is tossed about in reference to haircuts, new shoe fashions, and extremely rich desserts. When I say I love Kirk, I mean that I'm *in love* with Kirk and Lulu better watch her back. He's the reason I keep showing up in Stars Hollow for my weekly fix of quirk and whimsy, and he's the reason I'm chucking the Big Apple to move to the Nutmeg State.

The other people in Stars Hollow are fine enough, albeit a little dull next to the man of my dreams. Take Lorelai Gilmore, for instance. She's cool in a funky T-shirt-wearing, junk-food-eating, witty-joke-cracking sort of way. We could be buddies. Not best friends or anything. But the kind of acquaintances who show up at the same parties, air kiss, and promise that we'll get together for lunch soon then never do. I admire the raw pig-headed tenacity it must take to remain the rebel in her family for as long as she has. Then again, how hard could it be to stay at odds with the likes of straight-laced Emily and Richard? Lorelai's family is nothing compared to Kirk's. Growing up the youngest of twelve brothers and sisters in a bedroom with no windows—now that'll make a person a true individual.

Then there's Lorelai's daughter Rory, an absolute doll. She's the kind of gal you want to know. Someone you can sit down to discuss Gore Vidal's latest tome or Vidal Sassoon's latest mousse. So she felt like an outsider at Chilton, always straddling the line between the bitchy rich cliques and her working-class lifestyle back in Stars Hollow. She claims she's not a joiner, and Lorelai says she hates how such snotty private schools try to stamp out every vestige of individuality in the students. Yet compared to Kirk's secondary experience, Rory might as well have attended Smurfy Smurf's High School of Happiness. As he told her once, "I carried a duffle bag and ate lunch by myself everyday and I turned out just fine" ("Like Mother, Like Daughter," 2-7). I rest my case. Everyone finds his or her niche in life, and Rory's doing just dandy as an Ivy Leaguer these days.

There are other people in town I'd like to get to know. I could handle a passing, nod-and-smile, how-you-doing, nice-weather-we're-having kind of rapport with Luke Danes. Although he is an emotional wreck. Anyone who pines away for six years over someone else, like he did for Lorelai, then blows the whole thing right before they're supposed to get married... can we say baggage? You'd need a sky cap just to hang out with him. Jackson and Sookie would be on my list of People to Befriend. Who better to mooch from during festive eating holidays than a klutzy chef and her eggplant-serenading husband?

Heck, I wouldn't even mind knowing Taylor Doose. He might be an uptight pain in the patootie half the time, but you've got to hand it to him, he keeps things together in that town. Mussolini may have been a madman, but the trains always ran on time. Without Taylor, there'd be no movies in the town square, no Revolutionary War re-enactments, and no Festival of Living Art. Those things are half the fun of living in a small town where everybody knows your name. And your birthday. And what you had for dinner last night, who you had it with, and whether or not you're sleeping together.

Of course, before I begin the slow dance of seduction for my one true heart, my soul mate, the cock of the walk, if you will, I'll have to ingratiate myself to Babette and Miss Patty. Two old-school cronies dishing the dirt like the Louella Parsons and Hedda Hopper of Stars Hollow, without the cat fight, of course. Plus, those two have been around the block, if you know what I mean.

I think I could learn a few lessons about l'amour from Miss Patty. Who can resist a chain-smoking former showgirl and serial divorcee teaching the town's littlest blossoms the choreography to Swan Lake? She'll tell it like it is. "Come on, girls! Love waits for no one," I've heard her admonish her tiny ballerinas as they flit across the stage ("Hammers And Veils," 2-2). And she should know. Married four times to three men. Even in grief, before Fran's funeral, I heard her tell Lorelai, "It's times like these that you realize what's important in life. I'm so glad I had all that sex" ("Say Goodnight, Gracie," 3-20). (Sheesh, if it weren't for Miss Patty's lascivious ways, you'd begin to think Lorelai's constant bed-hopping was kind of slutty.)

Then there's Babette Dell. The way she tells it, she hoed some tough rows before settling down with Morey. "It's so hard being a woman," she's said. "You got your morals, standards, and your good common sense, then BAM you meet some guy and it all goes out the window" ("Help Wanted," 2-20). (Hmmm, sound familiar, Rory?) You've heard the stories from Babette—once a guy pushed her out of a moving car and she even joined a cult for another man. Found herself wearing a muumuu and banging a tambourine in an airport. Not that it's all that surprising. Babette is the one who lives with cats and garden gnomes for a family, in a house with big barn doors and tiny furniture.

Speaking of alternative living arrangements, some people may find it questionable that Kirk continues to live with his mother, but I think it's nice. You don't find that kind of filial piety outside of rural China anymore. Sure, there's Lorelai and Rory shacking up together next door to Babette, but let's admit it, they're just a few years shy of crossing that line from cute, single mom and her adorable wunderkind to full-blown Big and Little Edie serenading the raccoons at old Grey Gardens.

Oh, alright, I'll admit that Kirk may have his peculiarities, but on the whole he is steadfast and strong. Oh, I get prickly just thinking about him! What's not to love about Kirk? The man is good and kind and decent. Remember Cat Kirk? Few people, not even Babette the consummate cat lover, would have stuck it out so long with such a feisty feline, but Human Kirk was willing to go to the mat for his misunderstood mouser. He's also industrious and not afraid to take risks in his entrepreneurial pursuits. Lorelai and Sookie might have gone out on a limb to start the Dragonfly Inn, but that's nothing compared to Kirk's forays into Hay There lotion, topical headline T-shirts (Babette really did eat oatmeal!), retro bath mats, and one-of-a-kind hand-carved mailboxes (Condi Rice's mouth has never been so useful).

Kirk's the kind of guy who owns a town handbook, is not afraid to use a bullhorn to keep a buffet line moving, and takes the agreement between video store owner and video store customer seriously. Kirk might consider Taylor his mentor, but Taylor seems like a Merry Prankster flipping the bird at authority next to Kirk's resolute adherence to the rules. Some people might say those traits make one strict or inflexible or perhaps despotic and tyrannical, but I call it integrity and respect for tradition. There's nothing more seductive than a strong man who knows how to use his power. "Rumstud" might do it for some women, but Kirk's my man.

Then there's the softer side of Kirk. He's good looking in a Cary Grant meets Foghorn Leghorn's nemesis the baby chicken hawk sort of way. A creative genius who loves dance. When he blew out his knees from years of tap dancing he simply redirected his artistic energy into other pursuits. I'd say he was unparalleled as the director of Miss Patty's one-woman-show "Buckle Up, I'm Patty," even if the cast was a bit volatile. Then again, every Werner Herzog has his Klaus Kinski, and that tension simply makes better art. Kirk's own acting aspirations have led him to such seminal roles as the Woman of Questionable Morals who saves Stars Hollow from British invasion; a very convincing Server at the Bracebridge Dinner (who only broke character to defend the memory of *I Love Lucy* after Lorelai persisted in baiting him); and let's not forget the Giant Hot Dog who passed out flyers to promote lunch at the Dragonfly Inn (I know I was hungry just looking at him). Judging by his commitment to character when he played Christ in the staging of the Last Supper during the Festival of Living Art, I think it's clear that his particular genius leans toward Stasbergian Method Acting à la Pacino and De Niro.

Despite his live performance accomplishments, his true artistic brilliance was showcased during his directorial debut at Movie in the Square Night. *A Film by Kirk* will surely go down as a Stars Hollow instant classic. Asaad Kelada eat your heart out, man! Kirk has mad talent.

And he's loaded. Did I mention that? Luke Danes might consider himself the hardest working man in Stars Hollow, but slinging hash behind a lunch counter is nothing compared to 15,000 odd jobs over eleven years. Kirk's work ethic coupled with stupendous feats of frugality (he's a man who'll haggle over the price of a used book at a charity event) plus the miracle of compound interest have left Kirk a wealthy man, indeed. I'm not after his money, though. I'd sign a prenup in a heartbeat if that would seal the deal for him. I'd even let him have a spider monkey.

Frankly, I'm surprised that there isn't more competition for Kirk's affection. (Lorelai had her chance, but she turned up her snub little nose at his entreaty for her love.) He's obviously the most unique person to come out of Stars Hollow in a long time. Without his idiosyncrasies serving as the barometer of quirky in a small town full of oddballs, other people of Stars Hollow might start to seem a little strange, maybe even off-putting. But with Kirk around, no matter what other people do, they seem pretty normal.

The only problem I foresee in my romantic pursuit is how to woo a man with so much life experience. It's not as if I can jump out of an airplane trailing a sign professing my love. Kirk's already been a promotional parachutist, so my attempt would be mere parody. Whatever I do, it'll have to be something original and distinctive, because Kirk is truly one-of-a-kind. As he once told Lorelai, "Whimsy goes with everything!" ("An Affair To Remember," 4-6). I'm just hoping it'll go with me.

Heather Swain is the author of two novels, *Eliot's Banana* and *Luscious Lemon*, and the editor of *Before: Short Stories About Pregnancy*. Her fiction and nonfiction have appeared in literary journals, Web sites, and magazines. She lives in Brooklyn, New York, with her husband, two children, and dog.

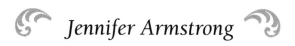

Jennifer Armstrong

Boys Not Allowed

LUKE: Will you marry me?
LORELAI: What?
LUKE: Just looking for something to shut you up. ("Kiss and Tell," 1-7)

Lorelai Gilmore had trouble staying engaged long enough to get married (the first smart thing Christopher did in the series was keep the engagement short) and Jennifer Armstrong knows why. If you have it all without saying, "I do," isn't it smarter to say, "I don't"?

T WAS WHEN MY PROFESSIONAL LIFE took a jolting upswing that I started questioning whether I wanted to go through with the wedding I'd been planning to the longtime love of my life. And that's no coincidence. I'd spent most of the decade that I'd been dating my fiancé pining for his proposal: I would write vows in my head, pick songs for our first dance—and because I am, at heart, an overachiever, I plowed through the wedding plans with determination once he finally popped the question.

Then I landed my dream job at *Entertainment Weekly* magazine—and, worse, I started to find my groove there, landed cover story assignments, got promoted. Worse still, I began making friends in the media and literary world of New York City, which put me in regular company with powerful editors and agents and authors who seemed to take my writing ambitions seriously. It occurred to me that I could do even more than be a staff writer at a national magazine. It occurred to me that I could be exactly the kind of person I'd barely dared to dream I could be—the kind of person who would've both fascinated and terrified the girl I was back in college. The girl I was when I met my fiancé. The girl I had absolutely no interest in even remembering anymore, much less being.

So I postponed the wedding I'd wanted for my entire adult life. And, eventually, I canceled it.

Since then, I have watched (on the television in my very writerly East Village studio that symbolizes my hard-won independence, natch) with particularly rapt attention as one Lorelai Gilmore first put off naming a wedding date when she got engaged to her presumed soulmate, Luke Danes…and then used her stunning organizational proficiency to plan the perfect wedding in record time…and then let him postpone it when things got complicated between them…and then called the whole thing off. Granted, she bolted because she was tired of waiting around for him to straighten out his relationship with the long-lost daughter who had recently resurfaced. But this wasn't the first time she'd reneged on an engagement—she literally skipped town on a previous wedding. And, heck, she couldn't even fully commit to Christopher *after* she'd impulsively married him on their trip to France.

I thought that if I examined her fictional wishy-washing closely enough, I might gain some real insight into my own waffling. I have, after all, always related to her stubbornness, her *joie de vivre*, and her passion for junk food. At least those first two traits ought to translate into a certain ability to make relationships work—to stick to them and to make the best of them, no matter what.

And yet both of us have become synonymous—her to *Gilmore Girls* fans, me to my own circle of friends—with the very twenty-first century phenomenon of female cold feet.

I've now realized it wasn't those aforementioned traits, but some other shared qualities that prompted both Lorelai and me to shiver in our stilettos: namely, that we're successful business women (she runs an inn with her best friend; aside from my day job, I run a Web site with my best friend) without biological clocks (she's got her kid; I've no interest in one). She lives in the feminist "wishful-thinking world," as the *Village Voice* called it, dreamed up by creator Amy Sherman-Palladino, where single moms raise brilliant daughters and men are nothing more than trifling distractions. I live in a post-feminist world that kicked in after the advent of *Gilmore Girls*, a place where Maureen Dowd asks *Are Men Necessary?* and we answer, "Not really." Modern girls may not talk as fast as the Gilmore Girls or engage in witty repartee with colorful townsfolk, but as far as female empowerment goes, we're catching up fast.

Yes, behind the pop culture references and the picturesque setting lurks a militant girls-rule ideology rivaled only by the likes of *Thelma & Louise*. Ally McBeal and Murphy Brown struck blows for strong-yet-neurotic single moms, *Sex and the City* single-handedly advanced female sexuality by about eight decades, and *Buffy the Vampire Slayer* and *Alias* gave us women who kicked ass quite literally. But *Gilmore Girls* is the one show that depicts the place Thelma and Louise would've gladly driven off a cliff to get to.

And women like me are transforming from must-snag-a-man drones into fully realized Lorelais (and Rorys).

To wit: Colleges now are brimming with overachieving little Rory Gilmores, as women now outnumber *and* outperform their male counterparts. The *Gilmore* world, however, exaggerates the gap to the extreme; in Stars Hollow, men lag to an astonishing extent. Rory's on-again, off-again flame Logan comes off as whip smart (their snappy banter gives them a crackling chemistry she never could've dreamed of with ex Dean)—but he prefers to rest on his wealth. "So that's what hard work feels like," he cracked after helping Rory with a school newspaper emergency. "Apparently I've been avoiding it for a reason" ("Friday Night's Alright for Fighting," 6-13).

Luke, on the other hand, couldn't even believe his long-lost daughter turned out super-smart—he bought *Geometry for Dummies* in an attempt to relate to her, only to find he didn't even understand *that*. And, incidentally, that daughter came to him only so she could use his DNA in a science fair project; she and her mother wanted neither money nor contact with him. Fathers are curiously useless all around, in fact: Rory's father, Christopher, stopped flaking on the Girls and started providing only after he inherited a huge fortune from his grandfather (thank goodness he didn't actually have to work for it). And Rory's best friend, Lane, apparently does have a father—but he's literally invisible, never to be seen on screen. We've met only her outrageously overbearing mom.

In fact, the only solid father figure around is Lorelai's father, Richard. He and Lorelai's mother, Emily, stand for traditional gender values, with Richard unable to let go of his business even after retirement and Emily positively wallowing in frivolously "female" pursuits—organizing cocktail parties and trolling social registers. It just so happens that Lorelai's relationship with her parents has always been strained—as has Logan's with his traditional, still-married parents, as has Lane's with her parents. A show that was borne from a partnership between its original network, the WB, and the Family Friendly Programming Forum has turned out to be one of the most subversively anti-marriage series around.

Heck, even upstanding Emily recognizes the downside of her traditionally proper life: "I've never done anything," she said during a rare humble moment, after watching Lorelai take a business call. A few moments later, she explained to Rory, "I was just admiring your mother's life" ("Scene in a Mall," 4-15).

There is, of course, plenty to admire about Lorelai's life—and that's precisely the point. She's gorgeous. She has a great daughter, with whom she's had a (mostly) enviable relationship. She owns an inn, and she has no shortage of caring (if quirky) friends. And despite living in a tiny town, she's enjoyed a fairly constant string of desirable suitors—not that she needs them, given everything else she has going for her.

That's what trips her up with every romance, from Christopher (her star-crossed love since she conceived Rory at sixteen) to Max (the perfectly nice teacher she bailed on after accepting his proposal) to Luke: because she doesn't *need* a man for anything, it's impossible for her to settle on one she wants for good, forever. You could argue that she simply doesn't want to put up with Luke's crap—namely, his insistence on keeping Lorelai and his daughter in virtually separate worlds. You could argue that she's simply meant to end up with Christopher. But I would argue that she's a typical ultra-modern woman, just like me: when you've gotten everything—or even more than—you've ever wanted, it's hard to figure where one decent-but-fallible guy fits in.

That's why it can feel so wrong, even when it's right: "I've never been married because it's not easy and I usually freak out and screw everything up," Lorelai told Rory after finishing all the planning for her wedding to Luke. "But I haven't freaked out about Luke yet. Why haven't I freaked out about Luke yet?...What if all the signs are saying things shouldn't be this easy, that I shouldn't get the guy I want?" ("The Perfect Dress," 6-11).

Lorelai Gilmore is what's wrong with so many modern relationships.

And yet, like in so many modern relationships, it's the guys who ultimately take the blame—or at least bring nothing but bad fortune to otherwise perfectly put-together girls—in Stars Hollow. Who wrecked Lane's chances at rock stardom with her band, Hep Alien? Her guitarist boyfriend, Zack, who had an onstage meltdown (because he was emotional about a fight they'd had) when record scouts came to see them play. And how did Rory find herself in the biggest mess of her young life? Logan—at least according to Mama Gilmore. "Let's take an inventory of all the delightful things that have happened since you waltzed into my daughter's life," Lorelai huffed when he asked her for help winning Rory back. "She was arrested, convicted, she's on probation, she'll have a criminal record unless we can get it expunged, she dropped out of school, moved out of my house, she didn't speak to me for five months, three weeks, and sixteen days" ("Just Like Gwen and Gavin," 6-12).

The Gilmore Girls are simply too busy, too driven, too perfect to allow themselves to be messed up by mere mortal men. As characters, they don't realize it, and they're susceptible to masculine charms like the rest of us, but that's what it comes down to, and—go figure—it's a male character who finally figured it out. "Let's just stop fighting it, okay?" Luke said to Lorelai during a profoundly sad post-breakup grocery store run-in. "You go back to being Lorelai Gilmore, and I'll go back to being the guy in the diner who pours your coffee" ("That's What You Get, Folks, For Makin' Whoopee," 7-2).

It's hard to decide these days, when so much of the world is ours to conquer: Do we just want a guy in the diner to pour our coffee, or do we have room for more from the men in our lives?

Jennifer Armstrong is a staff writer at *Entertainment Weekly* and the co-founder of alternative online women's magazine SirensMag.com.

References

Press, Joy. "The Sunshine Girls." *Village Voice*. 25 Oct. 2004. <http://www.villagevoice.com/arts/0443,tv,57816,27.html>.

Marklein, Mary Beth. "College Gender Gap Widens." *USA Today*. 19 Oct. 2005. <http://www.usatoday.com/news/education/2005-10-19-male-college-cover_x.htm>.

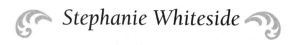

Stephanie Whiteside

When Paris Met Rory

PARIS: We're friends?
RORY: I'm not sure if there is an exact definition for what we are, but I do think it falls somewhere in the bizarro friends-ish realm. Come on, stay.
PARIS: Okay. But if you're doing all this so you can freeze my bra, I'll kill you. ("There's the Rub," 2-16)

They fight, they bicker, they banter, they break up and get back together again, they're a great couple, says Stephanie Whiteside. Lorelai and Luke? Nope, Rory and Paris, one of the most problematical relationships ever to grace a television series.

OR A SMALL, PEACEFUL TOWN in New England, there sure are a lot of complicated relationships in Stars Hollow. Luke and Lorelai. Rory and Dean. Rory and Jess. And those are just the romantic relationships. Let's not forget the strained peace between Lorelai and her parents. Or Lane and Mrs. Kim. Not to mention how Lorelai and Rory's mother-daughter bond, while occasionally idyllic, is anything but traditional. Yet none of those quite live up to the fascinating dynamic of the often uneasy and always entertaining relationship between Paris Gellar and Rory Gilmore.

At first glance, Paris and Rory appear to be an unlikely pair. From their first meeting at Chilton to their rocky roommate relationship, they spend almost as much time fighting as they do friends. But in many ways, Rory and Paris are two sides of the same coin. Both are extremely intelligent, motivated girls with big dreams. While they excel in the academic areas of life, and are very mature for their ages, neither one has the greatest social skills. Paris's caustic wit and competitive nature offend nearly everyone she comes in contact with and Rory prefers the company of her books to that of her classmates. And while both girls do have relationships, they seem to stumble into them more than actively pursue them, at least in the earlier seasons. Dean was the one to approach Rory, who was clearly astonished by the move, and Paris didn't even realize that Jamie had asked her out until Rory pointed it out to her. The similarities, however, end there—Rory comes across as being well-adjusted, if somewhat quirky, and is the perfect image of the girl next door. Paris, on the other hand, is often rude, mean, and more than a little bit neurotic. She is, in fact, what Rory could easily have become, had she been raised in Hartford, in the way her grandparents would have approved of. But Paris Gellar is more than a cautionary tale. Rory might not see it, but Paris may be the best thing that's ever happened to her.

Paris vs. Rory

But let's start at the beginning: Chilton. Paris and Rory's first meeting was filled with unexpected mishaps—and it was far from love at first sight. Paris immediately identified Rory as someone to be intimidated; Paris was number one at Chilton and she wasn't going to take the risk of anyone jeopardizing that. Rory's reaction was to be expected—after Paris's welcome, she wanted nothing more than to avoid her. But fate clearly wasn't going to let that happen. The two girls were thrown together in almost every class, and when Rory accidentally destroyed Paris's history project, the stage was set for major competition.

What Paris found when she met Rory was something unexpected—an equal adversary. Paris may have been low on Chilton's social hierarchy, but she was at the top of the academic world, and she knew it. Most of the other students already knew to steer clear of her temper, and from their first meeting she clearly expected Rory to crumble in the face of intimidation. Rory was also used to being number one—but she wasn't used to being challenged on it. Given what we've seen of Stars Hollow, it's easy to assume that Rory didn't have much in the way of academic competition at Stars Hollow High. Intimidation isn't Rory's style, but she was clearly thrown at being faced with someone whose drive and intelligence rivaled her own, and she didn't handle it much better than Paris.

The other striking similarity between them that first season was the maturity they displayed, much of which could be attributed to them being raised in a world consisting primarily of adults. Paris was clearly very attached to her nanny, and, from the impressive list of extracurriculars that she lorded over Rory, it appeared that most of her free time was taken up with school and résumé-building activities. Her only friends were Madeline and Louise, who hung out with Paris, one imagines, largely from habit. It certainly wasn't shared interests; Madeline and Louise were more concerned with the latest lipstick color or potential boyfriend to pay much attention to what was going on in Paris's life. Rory's situation wasn't that much different. At her birthday party in the first season, Lane Kim was the only other teenager present. Rory's friendship with Lane was, and some might say is, very close (much closer than Paris's with Madeline and Louise) but limited by Mrs. Kim and her many rules. The rest of the guests were the Stars Hollow residents with whom Rory spent most of her time. Her best friend, after all, is her mother—an adult. It's not surprising then, that both Rory and Paris ended up as bookish teens who related better to adults than their peers.

So how did Rory and Paris end up so different? Part of it must be attributed to the types of the adults they were surrounded by. The residents of Stars Hollow are far removed from the pressure-filled world of upper-class Hartford. Rory, unlike Paris, didn't need to earn the love of Stars Hollow. She had it, simply for being Rory. Paris was constantly trying to measure up, to be number one in everything she did. The standards Hartford society sets are, according to Chilton's Headmaster Charleston in "The Deer Hunters" (1-4), impossible to meet, but Paris tried anyway.

Paris also learned to be self-sufficient in a way that Rory didn't. Stars Hollow provided a support system that Rory could rely on in any situation. Even if she was fighting with Lorelai, she had Luke, Miss Patty, Sookie, and even Taylor looking out for her. She didn't have to develop the tough exterior Paris did, and so shows her emotions much more easily, whether over a missed test or failed Puffs initiation.

In later seasons, the extent of their similarities became obvious: after Rory dropped out of Yale, she and Paris went through a startling role reversal. All of a sudden Rory was face to face with Hartford society pressure, while Paris, suddenly broke, became the one who was working and spending her free time in Stars Hollow with Lorelai. From the Huntzbergers to the DAR, Rory finally stepped fully into the world Lorelai was so desperate to shield her from, the world Rory had been flirting with since the show's beginning—the world Paris grew up in. Estranged from her mother, Rory's steadiest sources of support were her grandparents, whose indulgence lasted only so long as they could control and mold Rory into the girl they wanted her to be, the girl Lorelai should have been, and Logan, whose family let her know in no uncertain terms that she didn't measure up, socially or professionally.

The first real fissures in her relationship with her grandparents came when Richard discovered she hadn't been reading at all, but rather focusing her energies on planning DAR social functions, in part (though not only) to make Emily happy. Rory, given her desire to please, would have suffered being raised under her grandparents' conflicting expectations; though she eventually returned to Yale as Richard wanted, it was a stubbornness and rebellious self-direction inherited from Lorelai that allowed her to break away from the life she was living and return to the one she'd wanted for herself. It's easy to imagine a Rory without Lorelai's influence—one who might have turned out little different than Paris, internalizing parental expectations she was bright enough to almost meet, but never truly satisfy.

Friendship

Their differences actually turn out to be much less crucial to the course of their relationship than their similarities do. If they weren't so much alike, Paris and Rory wouldn't spend so much time at each other's throats—but they also wouldn't be such good friends.

No character exists in a bubble, and Paris and Rory each had friends before the other came along. They might have been as different as night and day, but Louise and Madeline stuck by Paris during their time at Chilton. Despite being boy-crazy and more than a little flighty, Louise and Madeline were loyal friends. They never made a move on Paris's crush, Tristan, even though he's just the type of guy they would normally have gone after. And even though Rory and Madeline seemed to be forming a tentative friendship, Madeline was quick to ignore Rory when Paris and Rory were fighting. Yet Paris's friendship with the two clearly didn't run very deep, and after Chilton Louise and Madeline virtually disappeared. At Yale, Paris was never seen with any friends other than Rory, and her only other consistent companion was her on-again, off-again boyfriend Doyle.

Rory's support system has consisted largely of Lorelai and Lane. Lorelai is both mother and best friend, something that works out surprisingly well, on the whole. Lorelai clearly doesn't understand the complicated friendship between Paris and Rory, but makes every effort to be supportive, whether by hating Paris on Rory's behalf, or inviting her to stay at the Independence Inn or go to a Bangles concert when they are getting along. Rory also has Lane, the only person her own age that, in high school at least, Rory seemed to be friends with (not counting Dean or Jess, both of whom were newcomers to Stars Hollow). Lane and Rory started out as close friends, but their friendship started to deteriorate after Rory transferred to Chilton. Lane may be Rory's best friend, but Rory is almost completely unaware of what is going on in her life. Even that first year at Chilton, Rory knew more about Paris—her supposed enemy—than she did her best friend.

Like it or not, Paris and Rory have much more in common with each other than they do with any of their other friends. Louise, Madeline, Lane, and even Lorelai don't really understand the intensity and drive that both Rory and Paris possess. Lane and Rory bond over music, but it's hard to imagine Lane discussing Kafka or Tolstoy with Rory. Louise and Madeline have even less in common with Paris. Given the circumstances, it seems like Paris and Rory should have been instant friends. Neither had anyone else in their life who shared so many interests and qualities. But life is never that easy. Paris is too competitive to let anyone stand in her way, and she's not going to waste time getting to know her competition first. Between Paris's competitive streak and Rory's disastrous first day at Chilton, they were off to a rocky start. But thanks to what occasionally felt like a Chilton-wide conspiracy to force them into the same group for one class project or another (even Headmaster Charleston went out of his way to force the two of them to cooperate), Paris and Rory couldn't escape the fact that they were going to have to work together. And eventually, they began to thaw.

The Bangles concert is the first time that we saw real overtures of friendship, but given Paris's mercurial temper, the friendly periods between the two never lasted for long. Without meaning to, Rory continually made the relationship worse. She set Paris up with Tristan without telling her—a nice thought, but one that blew up in her face. Rory outshone Paris without even trying to, and all of Paris's hard work only left her alone and frustrated. Rory had a boyfriend and supportive family. Rory got into the Puffs without even knowing who they were and Paris, who had been trying to do the same for years, was forced to ask for Rory's help. Paris invited Rory to be her VP in the student council race so that Paris would get enough votes to win, and then became paranoid that Rory was going to take over. Hardly a surprise, considering that most of the other council members seemed to like Rory better than Paris. All of this must have come as an incredible blow to Paris, who put much more effort into these things than Rory. The worst part must have been Rory's refusal to acknowledge that the two were even competing.

This sort of upstaging didn't stop at Chilton—Rory got into Harvard and decided not to go, while Paris didn't even get in. Not surprisingly, the academic competition cooled a bit once they arrived at Yale. With Rory majoring in journalism and Paris in pre-med, it was unlikely they would have many classes together. But even there, Rory stole Paris's thunder. When Paris was made editor of the *Yale Daily News*, her micro-managing determination to be the best only drove away the staff and, just like with the student council at Chilton, the students that remained turned to Rory. Everyone seemed to realize that Rory was the only person who could really get through to Paris—everyone except Rory, that is. Rory was reluctant to interfere, but when Paris finally snapped she had no other choice. Rory wasn't angling to be the next editor, but she ended up with the job anyway.

But in between these spurts of competition, Paris and Rory have managed to be amazingly supportive of each other. When Paris appeared as Rory's roommate at Yale, it came as a complete shock to Rory, but she never suggested changing rooms and ended up living with Paris the year after, as well. Rory's the one who showed up at the hospital for Paris when Asher Flemming collapsed, and she was the one who found Paris a job when Paris found out she was broke. Paris is equally supportive of Rory, in her own way. She covered for Rory when Dean found Jess at the Gilmores', convincing Dean that

Jess was only there because of Paris's crush on him. She also pushed Rory at Chilton and attempted to convince her to come back to Yale when she decided to take some time off, something Rory eventually saw the wisdom of. When both girls found themselves suddenly dumped and single, they wound up sharing a sketchy apartment and wallowing together.

A Perfect Match

Paris had more trouble allowing herself to become friends with Rory, but she has also ended up appreciating it more. For the most part, Rory just seems to tolerate Paris; she doesn't seem to place as high a value on the relationship. After Chilton, Rory seemed content to forget about her. It was Paris (with the help of her life coach) who requested to be Rory's roommate at Yale. While she considers Paris a friend, Rory isn't the one seeking the relationship out; Paris is. Paris even admitted to Lorelai that she was lost without Rory. She was speaking academically, but her words hold true for more than that.

In fact, friends doesn't seem to be quite the right word to describe people wanting to strangle each other with the nearest rope-like object. But they aren't enemies, either, and haven't been since they set aside the animosity from their first months together at Chilton. They are roommates, on and off, but that term also doesn't convey the extent of their relationship. If it weren't for the lack of sex, I would say the best way to describe their relationship would be soul mates.

Yes, soul mates.

Although they are completely platonic (drunken spring break kisses notwithstanding), Paris and Rory's friendship has all the elements of a great relationship. They are alike enough to get along, but different enough to challenge each other. Their relationship, from the awkward beginning to the series of misunderstandings, fights, and mishaps that followed, has all the makings of a classic romantic comedy.

Paris and Rory have a lot to learn from each other. With Rory, Paris has permission to relax. Not just in the literal sense, by going to Bangles concerts and eating mac and cheese, but by having a place where she can be herself. Rory understands Paris in a way that Madeline and Louise never did or could. She understands that rereading *The Iliad* isn't doing nothing, and that watching *The Power of Myth* can be just as much fun as a spring break party.

Rory has a few things to learn from Paris, too. Rory's life in Stars Hollow was idyllic, probably too much so. In order to make it in the real world, and especially the world of journalism, she's going to have to develop a much thicker skin. Competing with Paris has prepared her to handle herself in a world where just being nice and smart isn't enough to succeed.

Paris and Rory challenge each other, something that is missing from the other relationships they have. Dean was awed by Rory's intelligence, and he supported her but he couldn't push her. Jess was much more Rory's intellectual equal, but he was too unpredictable and emotionally distant. Logan has arguably been the most compatible of Rory's boyfriends, but if anyone has been challenged in that relationship, it's him. Paris dates even less than Rory, going out with Asher Flemming, who she worshipped without question, and Doyle, who simply bends to her will.

Imagine what could happen if Paris and Rory put their differences aside, agreed to stop competing, and managed to be supportive of each other at the same time. They've come close with the *Yale Daily News* and the Chilton student government, where they made a great team—Paris provided the pressure to perform, and Rory brought people skills and the ability to see the big picture.

Together, Paris and Rory would be an unstoppable couple. All they'd have to do is realize it.

And maybe reconsider the whole no-sex thing.

Stephanie Whiteside recently graduated from The George Washington University with a BA in political communication, where she learned the fine art of procrastination by watching *Gilmore Girls* and knitting when she should have been writing papers. Stephanie currently lives in Northern Virginia with her cats Fred and Padma, and spends her time watching more TV than is probably healthy, writing, and attempting to convince the government to give her a job. In the meantime, she teaches knitting and is cleverly disguised as a responsible adult.

The Other Relationship: Parenting

Janine Hiddlestone

Mothers, Daughters, and Gilmore Girls

LORELAI: It's from my mother.
RORY: What is it?
LORELAI: It's heavy. Must be her hopes and dreams for me.
RORY: I thought she discarded those years ago. ("Dear Emily and Richard," 3-13)

The bond between mother and daughter is a strong one, and no show has ever explored it in so many ways through so many generations and so many traditions as *Gilmore Girls*. Janine Hiddlestone looks at them all as she analyzes the fears, disappointments, and triumphs of mothering in Stars Hollow.

"YOUR FIRST COP-RAIDED PARTY. I am just so proud!" gushes Lorelai Gilmore to her daughter, Rory. Upon discovering just moments later that a fight between two boys over Rory is what resulted in the arrival of the police, Lorelai breaks into the chorus of *The Wind Beneath My Wings* ("Did you ever know that you're my hero, everything I longed to be . . ."). Rory stalks off in embarrassment and annoyance ("Say Goodnight, Gracie," 3-20).

It was an amusing scene, particularly since Lorelai continued to sing as she followed her daughter down the street—the fun sort of scene viewers of *Gilmore Girls* have come to expect. However, for the uninitiated, the scene had a few peculiarities. In most family/teen dramas or sitcoms (and in real life), the parent or parents would have been furious at their teenage daughter for attending a "parents out of town" keg party that ended when the police broke up a fight and dispersed the intoxicated party-goers. The fact that Rory was sober and ashamed would not have swayed most parents. There would have been lectures, exhortations of disappointment, and very likely a grounding. But this is *Gilmore Girls*, and the usual logic about parent-child interactions does not apply.

When Amy Sherman-Palladino created *Gilmore Girls*, which debuted in 2000, most dismissed it as another teen drama with family-friendly overtones—racier than *7th Heaven*, but more "value oriented" than *Dawson's Creek*. Its popularity, currently holding strong in the show's seventh season, belied the naysayers, as *Gilmore Girls* proved to be more than the paint-by-numbers show it appeared to be on the surface (Haberman). Behind the impossibly gorgeous leads, the teen angst, the romances, the breakups, the small town, and the family dramas was a surprisingly subversive undertone. The small town, though beloved, is portrayed satirically, poking fun at the stereotypes of small town characters and idealized life. There are the interfering locals and their inevitable gossiping, the white picket fences, and the too-good-to-be-true square with its picturesque pavilion, but everything also has a little twist. The hardware store is actually a diner run by a cantankerous softie, the mechanic is an unapologetically eccentric woman, the requisite antique store is owned by fundamentalist Christian Koreans, and festivals and town events seem to occur on almost a weekly basis: "Well, this is a town that likes the celebrating. Last year we had a month long carnival when we finally got off the septic tank system" Rory told Dean as the town prepared for the Stars Hollow Firelight Festival ("Star-Crossed Lovers and Other Strangers," 1-16). Dialogue is conducted largely through clever witticisms and fast-paced banter that incorporates everything from popular culture and literature to politics and social commentary. But the most refreshingly subversive element of all is the show's treatment of and focus on family dynamics. However, more than anything else, it is the relationship between the three (and sometimes four) generations of Gilmores—particularly the women—around which the stories and characters develop, and which comprises the real heart of the show.

Ostensibly, Lorelai is the quintessential unwed (and still single) mother made good. Since she ran away from home, pregnant, at sixteen, she has made it her purpose to prevent her daughter from making the same mistakes Lorelai did and therefore give her all the opportunities Lorelai missed out on in her own youth. But here is largely where this particular stereotype ends and the story begins to play against type. Lorelai's parents are wealthy socialites, and did not throw her out, even after the birth of her daughter Rory (though there is little doubt they drove her away). Upon running away, she took her newborn baby *from* the city to a seemingly conservative small town, where she was embraced by the townspeople and given work at the Independence Inn, a metaphor if ever there was one. By the time the first season began nearly sixteen years later, Lorelai was managing the prosperous establishment with a competence that belied her behavior away from work. Moreover, her attitude in regard to raising her daughter was to be the "cool mom": the best friend. While there is nothing unusual about the "cool mom" character in television shows, Lorelai takes it to a new level. While Rory was living at home, there was no punishment and few rules (with most of these appearing to be enforced by Rory), and the relationship was as close to equality as a parent-child relationship can get. Lorelai was in charge, but with Rory's permission:

RORY: The longer you wait the harder it's gonna be.
LORELAI: For the love of God, will you please ring the bell.
RORY: You can tell them before dinner.
LORELAI: I will tell them when I'm ready to tell them. You have to accept that because I'm the mother and you're the daughter, and in some cultures, that means you have to do what I say.
RORY: If you don't tell them in two weeks, I will.
LORELAI: Though apparently not in this one. ("Hammers And Veils," 2-2)

Rory was what many people would consider "the perfect daughter." She was kind, friendly, hard-working, well-mannered, über-smart, and remarkably well-behaved. Despite being a quiet bookworm, she somehow avoided being labeled a "geek," though it is never exactly clear where she fits socially. There was in fact an episode addressing this very issue in the second season, in which the Chilton headmaster attempted to force her into a group—any group, because "universities do not look kindly on loners" ("Like Mother, Like Daughter," 2-7). Her maturity defied her age, and more often than not she was presented as the "adult" in the mother-daughter relationship. Rory's occasionally exasperated tolerance of her mother's antics is amusing, and it is she who sometimes has to draw a line or even call a halt to proceedings.

> RORY: Usually I have to drag you out of here kicking and scream-
> ing to go to dinner.... You whine, you complain, you act like a
> child.
> LORELAI: I do not.
> RORY: I had to pay you five bucks once so you wouldn't go in sweats.
> (The Third Lorelai," 1-18)

This should not suggest that Lorelai is irresponsible or a bad mother; Rory herself is a reflection of Lorelai's parenting savvy, as is the high regard in which the rest of the town holds the pair. Clearly, the towns-people consider themselves to be surrogate parents to Rory, provid-ing stability, guidance, and care. They take a startling interest in her every step, attend all her birthdays, share her every joy and sorrow, and display a willingness to take up pitchforks if anyone hurts her (such as after the car accident with Jess). Nevertheless, ultimately it is Lorelai who must be given the credit, because perhaps most impor-tantly, love and affection are never in short supply.

It is not that Lorelai does not ever display any parental behavior; she can certainly be the "mother" instead of the "best friend" when necessary. This has been demonstrated in her refusal to lie to Lane's mother (the "mother's code"); her opposition to Jess's interest in Rory and her rampaging behavior after he crashed Rory's car; her anger and concern when Rory did not return until dawn after her first dance; and perhaps most impressively, when she dragged the two recalci-trant sixteen-year-olds she was chaperoning (Paris's friends Madeline and Louise) out of a wild party in an apartment in New York while Rory and Paris watched in wonder. Still, the vast majority of Lorelai and Rory's interactions are far from typical, and there are rarely reper-cussions to their unorthodox relationship except for the occasional argument, as Lorelai expects Rory to make mistakes and learn from them immediately...though in *Gilmore Girls*'s world, Rory generally does. The writers are of course aware of the discrepancy between this and the usual expectations for mother-daughter relationships, and cleverly highlight and poke gentle fun at the unusual relationship from time to time, even as early as the pilot episode, which helps to shave the edges of saccharine sweetness from the show. Lorelai's reaction to Rory's acceptance at the exclusive private school, Chilton, demonstrated the mocking wit fans would come to enjoy:

> This is it. She can finally go to Harvard like she's always wanted and get the education that I never got and get to do all the things that I never got to do and then I can resent her for it and we can finally have a normal mother-daughter relationship ("Pilot," 1-1).

Lorelai is such a good mother, her relationship with her daughter so thoroughly based on respect and equality, that upon being introduced to her parents, Richard and Emily, it is almost impossible to believe that she ever spent a day in their home, let alone was raised by them. They are New England aristocracy, complete with *Mayflower* and Revolutionary ancestry, with all of the traditions and history. They are wealthy, not simply through "old" family money, but also Richard's success in insurance. The house is a showpiece of vast, rarely used rooms, and although perfect for Emily's famous cocktail parties, the remainder of the time the house exudes an over-decorated austerity. It is difficult to imagine Lorelai being a child in that house; she seems out of place enough as an adult: her animated movements and even more energized personality seem stifled by—or dangerous to—the grand house. There are times when Lorelai's membership in the family seems to have been some mistake, as if the chauffer collected the wrong child from pre-school one day (one imagines they may have noticed if it happened in junior high). It is not even as if Lorelai was raised by servants, as it is clear that Emily was largely a hands-on mother; her need for control would allow nothing less. But as the show progresses, there are occasional glimpses of Emily in Lorelai, and more significantly, aspects of both Emily and Richard in Rory. She displays the best of her parents and grandparents; any other combination of their traits could have had a volatile, if not downright frightening, outcome, one that would have made Damien seem like a Brady.

It would be easy to assume that Lorelai was not loved enough, but that would be unfair. Displays of affection might have been rare, but love was obviously never an issue. Lorelai's parents would have given their child the world—she just didn't want the world they had to offer. Psychoanalysis aside, it becomes obvious that they simply agree on few things and have little in common—except Rory, of course—and compromise seems difficult for both Lorelai and her parents. It was Rory who reunited them after sixteen years of limited and infrequent contact (as Emily commented in the pilot: "Is it Easter already?"); the weekly visits were initially a condition of a loan to Lorelai for Rory's schooling, and Rory hit it off with her grandparents almost immediately. Lorelai's relationship with them, however, remained a little like the Middle East: volatile, plagued with frequent misunderstandings, and visited by periods of eerie calm. (Peace talks always end without clear resolutions and generally lead to bloodshed.) In a mostly light and amusing show, it is sometimes achingly sad—but remarkably realistic—to watch these three decent people repeatedly sabotage any improvement in their relationships. It is a credit to Rory that she has not succumbed to the urge to knock all their heads together—though one wonders if it might be worthwhile.

Rory is clearly more comfortable in her grandparents' world than her mother ever had been. Initially, her good relations with them could have been attributed to her politeness and attempts to make them happy (it seems Rory's mission in life to attempt to ensure everyone's happiness). However, it soon became obvious that it was no façade. The most obvious breakthrough came during Rory's trip with Richard to the Gilmores' country club. After the preliminary awkwardness, a conversation on travel broke the ice and they found mutual interests; suddenly everything changed. He introduced her to his friends with obvious pride, and she in turn made a good impression. By lunch they were sharing gossip and a firm relationship had been forged. Emily setting aside her pride and attending Rory's sixteenth birthday party had a similar effect, but although an affectionate relationship developed between them, they share no interests the way Richard and Rory do.

Lorelai was surprised at how quickly Rory bonded with her grandparents and put much of it down to Rory's good nature, as she was sure they were manipulating Rory in order to unsettle, or at least irritate, Lorelai:

EMILY: Well, isn't this interesting? You're afraid.

LORELAI: Of what?

EMILY: That Rory will enjoy the club and have a good time without you.

LORELAI: That's crazy.

EMILY: I agree.

LORELAI: I'm not afraid.

EMILY: Then let her go.

LORELAI: She won't enjoy it, Mom....Believe it or not, this is not about you.

EMILY: Of course it's about me. If Rory goes and has a good time without you, then I win. ("Kill Me Now," 1-3)

But it is the relationship between Rory and Richard that most perturbs her: she is even a little hurt and jealous. Lorelai's relationship with her mother has always been volatile, though they have their good moments, but it appears she is almost permanently estranged from her father. It is apparent that he has never known how to deal with her—talk to or interact with her—and his disappointment in her is palpable. To see him making such an effort with Rory is particularly galling. Although Lorelai and Richard's relationship has gradually improved (in tiny increments) over the ensuing years, it has never become completely comfortable. The problems were made particularly poignant as she rushed to his side when he was admitted to hospital:

LORELAI: I feel like this is one of those moments when I should be remembering all the great times I had with my dad, you know. The time he took me shopping for a Barbie or to the circus or fishing and my mind is a complete blank.

LUKE: Well I'm sure it happened.

LORELAI: No it didn't. We never did any of that. He went to work, he came home, he read the paper, he went to bed, I snuck out the window. Simple. He was a very by the numbers guy. I was never very good with numbers.

LUKE: I'm sure he loves you....

LORELAI: You know my dad is not a bad guy.

LUKE: I'm sure he's not.

LORELAI: He lived his life the way he thought he was supposed to. He followed the rules taught to him by his non-fishing-non-Barbie-buying dad. He worked hard. He bought a nice house. He provided for my mom. All he asked in return was for his daughter to wear white dresses and go to cotillion and want the same life that he had. What a disappointment it must have been for him to get me. ("Forgiveness and Stuff," 1-10)

It does not take a psychology major to realize that Rory is the daughter Richard and Emily had wanted—and expected, though never achieved—in Lorelai. Her direction in life, in addition to her quiet nature and eagerness to please, fits into their expectations: a prestigious private school; an Ivy League college. They were also particularly anxious that these plans not be derailed, as Lorelai's were, by a boyfriend, and all that might entail:

> LORELAI: I don't think my father has ever loved anything in this world as much as he loves you. Now, that having been established, let's just consider that maybe this flip-out tonight actually came from somewhere that possibly has nothing to do with Dean and very possibly has nothing to do with you.
> RORY: What are you talking about?
> LORELAI: You are the great white hope of the Gilmore clan. You are their angel sent from up above. You are the daughter they didn't have. ("Sadie, Sadie," 2-1)

Ironically, it is the tolerant and for the most part sensible upbringing provided by Lorelai that allows Rory to move easily between the world of her grandparents and the world of Stars Hollow. She willingly (if a little cautiously) takes part in events with her grandparents that Lorelai had been unwilling or unable to do, particularly demonstrated by the debutante ball and the Yale-Harvard football game. In fact, it could be suggested that her major acts of rebellion against her upbringing (i.e., her mother) generally involve her grandparents: dropping out of Yale, her relationship with Logan, perhaps even the above-mentioned social activities that her mother was so relieved to escape. The senior Gilmores have all but given up on Lorelai, instead pouring their hopes and dreams into Rory, but Rory rarely takes advantage of the situation. She asks nothing of them until her high school graduation when she approaches them for a loan to help pay for college. This was probably her most significant act of rebellion, even though it was done to assist Lorelai in fulfilling her dream of opening an inn of her own.

Rory spends considerable time and energy trying to keep the peace, or mend fences, between the generations, and despite all apparent evidence to the contrary, she has more success than she realizes. It is obvious that the relationships would have irreparably broken down without her continuing efforts, many of which must have been difficult for her, considering most appear to be grounded in her very existence. Nowhere was this more clearly demonstrated than at a dinner attended by mother Lorelai, father Christopher, and both sets of grandparents, where Lorelai's pregnancy at sixteen was touted as having ruined everybody's lives. Afterwards, both Lorelai and Emily worked to reassure Rory that she was not a mistake.

> EMILY: Rory, I know you heard a lot of talk about various disappointments this evening and I know you've heard a lot of talk about it in the past. But I want to make this very clear—you, young lady, your person and your existence have never ever been—not even for a second—included in that list. Do you understand me? ("Christopher Returns," 1-15)

Rory repeatedly claims to know and believe that, but some part of her must surely question it—particularly when it is so often raised. However, it becomes obvious over time—surely even to Rory—that Lorelai's problems with her parents date from well before Rory's conception and possibly as far back as Lorelai's. If anything, one wonders if it wasn't Rory's unexpected arrival that might have saved Lorelai by forcing her to be responsible and make a life for herself.

Of course, it should not be suggested that Rory is solely responsible for the good relationship she has with her grandparents, as it is apparent that they are more tolerant and make more of an effort with her than with Lorelai. While it is hardly unusual for grandparents to be more laid back with grandchildren, here it goes deeper and is much more complex. Though Emily in particular is perfectly willing to put Rory in her place or express dismay, not only is it rarely required, but neither Richard nor Emily approach Rory with suspicion or defensiveness, and aren't always looking for an ulterior motive. Any perceived failings in Rory are immediately attributed to Lorelai: "I don't understand how you could've been so irresponsible. It was your responsibility to stop this," Emily told Lorelai after Rory and Jess's car accident, appearing to miss the irony of the idea that a child's failings are the fault of the parents ("Help Wanted," 2-20). But whether they do so consciously or not, Richard and Emily are providing, if not a haven, then at least an alternative home (and not simply a physical space) for Rory, in the house where Lorelai felt excluded all those years ago. To her it had been a prison—not even a gilded cage—where appropriate attire and behavior were continually enforced. Therefore, it came as quite a shock to Lorelai to find that her daughter considered her grandparents as people to whom she could turn for help or comfort when Lorelai was unavailable. In fact, after a terrible argument with Rory, Lorelai was more distraught to discover Rory had gone all the way to her grandparents in Hartford then she was about the argument itself.

> RORY: I don't know. I just snapped and I got sick of everything. I
> wanted to go anywhere.
> LORELAI: So you picked hell?
> RORY: It was the first place that came to mind. ("P.S. I Lo...," 1-20)

She was downright disbelieving when Rory went to live there after dropping out of Yale. What made this event so extraordinary to Lorelai was that it was poor judgment and questionable behavior on Rory's part that led to the incident. Initially, Richard and Emily, as one would expect given their handling of Lorelai in her youth, agreed with Lorelai and promised to help—"Well, of course we'll back you up! This is not happening!" Emily told her—but they had a dramatic change of heart shortly after a visit from their granddaughter: "Rory is young. And I'm sure, once she's had some time and some space, she will change her mind. But for now, this is what she wants to do. And we need to respect that," Richard told a disbelieving Lorelai, who quite rightly felt betrayed ("A House is Not a Home," 5-22). That Rory has been arrested on a felony charge and then walked away from the education for which her grandparents had been paying did not prevent them from helping her—or supporting her decision. Certainly, Richard and Emily were far from happy and more than slightly disappointed, but they nevertheless stood by Rory in a manner in which they did not for Lorelai. In an astonishing reversal, Lorelai was the one who did not support Rory's abandonment of her education and was left to point out the error in her parents' judgment. Eventually Lorelai and Rory reconciled, and Rory, of course, returned to Yale, but the reversal of Lorelai and her parents' roles provided an interesting twist, while the anger and lack of contact between the two leads altered the shows dynamic throughout much of the sixth season. It was during this period that the similarities between Lorelai and her parents were most clear—and the similarities between Lorelai and Rory were most striking. Rory, the "perfect daughter," was not quite as perfect as Lorelai might have liked, and at first, Lorelai handled it little better than her mother had before her.

In fact, it was Rory's almost disturbingly good "child" behavior that made her "adult" behavior in seasons five and six (her affair with the married Dean, her brush with the law, and dropping out of Yale) so surprising and, indeed, shocking. Though it hardly matched the drama on *Melrose Place* or *Desperate Housewives*, it certainly dragged the show out of the tween market and, perhaps damagingly, away from its whimsical roots, dampening the humor somewhat as its characters struggled with the consequences of their choices.

The departure of creative team Amy Sherman-Palladino and Daniel Palladino at the end of the sixth season left some viewers concerned about the future direction of the show (Stewart). But while their departure may have meant sacrificing some of the show's signature pop culture-laden patter, it did not mean sacrificing its conceptual heart. Few shows have captured the good, the bad, and the downright ugly of family relationships with the poignancy and humor of *Gilmore Girls*. The key to the show is, as it has always been, its unorthodox—and through that, unexpectedly realistic—take on family dynamics; Richard, Emily, Lorelai, and Rory form one of the most interesting and intelligent families on television. And ultimately, they represent second chances (and third and fourth . . .); an opportunity to keep doing it again until you get it "right"—whatever that may be. Because, as Lorelai pointed out when told by Luke that she is a good mother, "Yeah, it's just the daughter part I don't have down yet" ("Forgiveness and Stuff," 1-10).

Janine Hiddlestone is a lecturer and tutor in politics, history, and communications at James Cook University in Australia. She has a Ph.D. in political history and has published on the place of war in culture and history, and how pop culture became the centerpiece of so much of the public's understanding—and misunderstanding—of events. She has explored the influence of technology on pop culture and vice versa, as well as its pedagogical uses in encouraging students to develop an interest in political and historical issues. She has also attained infamy among her colleagues as a pop culture tragic.

References

Haberman, Lia. "*Gilmore Girls*—Review." *E! Online*. Oct. 2000. <http://www.eonline.com/Features/Features/Tube2000/Shows/index2.html>.

Stewart, Sara. "Girls Gone Mild: Dumbing Down the Sassiest Family on Television" *The New York Post*, 15 Oct. 2006. <http://www.nypost.com/seven/10152006/entertainment/girls_gone_mild_entertainment_sara_stewart.htm>.

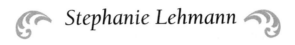

Stephanie Lehmann

The Best-Friend Mom

Rory: Oh my God, I hate her.
Lorelai: Ah, me too.
Rory: You have no idea who I'm talking about.
Lorelai: Solidarity, sister. ("Nick & Nora/Sid & Nancy," 2-5)

One of the biggest fantasies *Gilmore Girls* ever spun was that a mother and daughter could be best friends first, parent and child second, and it's one Stephanie Lehmann pays tribute to at the start of her essay. But sooner or later, she points out, no matter how hard you try to put it off, it's Mommy & Me time, even if you're Lorelai and Rory Gilmore.

THE SYMBIOTIC RELATIONSHIP between young, hip mom Lorelai and her preternaturally mature teenage daughter Rory is one of the big reasons I love watching *Gilmore Girls*. In the mornings they breakfast together at Luke's diner, where they gorge on huge meals like blueberry pancakes with bacon and eggs, sip oversized cups of coffee, and yak in fast-clipped language riddled with pop culture references. In the evenings there's take-out food in front of the TV and more yakking. In between, there's as little housework as humanly possible. Week after week, it's just the two of them enjoying the quirky charms of small-town life.

Perhaps I'm flattering myself, but I like to think my daughter and I share a similar bond. Okay, maybe I was well past high school when I gave birth to her, but I can still be marginally hip, right? I have a blog. I work out listening to an iPod. I allowed her to go on the pill at seventeen even though I would've preferred to lock her up in a chastity belt.

Perhaps the most fascinating aspect of the show has been the

chance to see Rory grow from an innocent fourteen-year-old virgin
to a sophisticated, sexually active twenty-one-year-old woman. And
it's always intriguing to see how Lorelai, the coolest of moms, handles the inevitable complications. Lorelai's relationship with her own
mother is fraught with conflict. Pregnant at sixteen, she left home
and raised Rory on her own. Lorelai needed distance from her parents' uptight, ostentatious lifestyle and their Mayflower-descended
values. Rejecting all their Eastern Establishment power and money,
she supported herself as a maid. Rory became the most important relationship in her life.

But the idyllic mother-daughter bubble pops—and the premise of
the show is established—when Lorelai finds herself drawn back into
the family fold. Rory wants to go to Chilton, a private high school
that will help pave the way to the Ivy League. Lorelai can't afford the
tuition. She reluctantly turns to her parents for financial help. Emily begins to take full advantage of her financial power to get closer
to Lorelai.

In one particularly revealing episode, Emily, in her typically manipulative way, offers Lorelai a trip to a spa. After Lorelai accepts,
Emily invites herself along. Once there, Emily won't leave Lorelai
alone. She even arranges for them to have a "couples' massage." Lorelai pretty much wards off that overture by pointing out that couples
massages are for "couples," not "a couple of people," and the couple
usually has sex together afterwards. By the end of the day, Emily's attempt to bond with Lorelai has failed miserably. Emily, on the verge
of tears, asks in a rather heartbreaking, childlike way, "Why can't we
have what you and Rory have?" ("There's the Rub," 2-16). Lorelai answers that she and Rory are "best friends first and mother and daughter second." Emily responds that she wasn't taught to be best friends
with her daughter; she was taught to be a "role model." Being a role
model means setting an example for someone else to follow. Considering that Lorelai tries as hard as she can to be different from her
mother, we'd have to say Emily has botched that one.

But is it possible to be your daughter's best friend? It's easy to see
the appeal. These days, boomer parents—in our quest to ward off old
age—are very into the idea of being close to our kids. We don't want
to be stuffy disciplinarians full of rules and old-fashioned ideas; we
want to be cool, understanding, and fun to hang out with. Plus, it's

hard to find best friends out there. So why not create a human being who can be your best buddy? She's handy, she's moldable, and more than anything in the world, you want what's best for her and she wants what's best for you. Right?

On the other hand, it sounds so Joan and Melissa Rivers. If the *Gilmore Girls* were to continue on for a few decades, I could see Lorelai desperately trying to stay young using every surgical procedure known to man. Rory would try to seem like the sane one without ever escaping her mother's shadow. Maybe there is such a thing as *too* close.

But still. It's a very seductive concept. Just turn on the opening credits and I get filled with that warm and fuzzy I-want-to-be-part-of-this picture feeling. I may be a city girl, but who needs Manhattan? Stars Hollow here I come. Heck, why did I ever get married? Give me a too-wise-for-her-years teenage daughter for company, an endless supply of donuts and videos, a diner with good coffee and a broad-shouldered hunk to pour it—I'd be happy.

And they are happy for the first few seasons. Sure, Lorelai has Friday night dinners with Richard and Emily to dread and their constant disapproval to live down. But Rory is always there as a buffer. Plus, Lorelai is doing just fine running the Independence Inn. The prodigal daughter has returned, and her past failures can be put behind her—especially since she has this daughter who is totally devoted to her and their somewhat wacky way of life.

But, as every woman knows, it's not easy to maintain that best-friend bond over time. And if that bond's between a mother and a daughter, it seems like it could be particularly tricky. Do you smoke your first cigarette with mom? Your first joint? Is she there to keep your hair out of your face while you're throwing up on the curb from your first vodka binge? Do you graduate to club hopping together like Lindsay Lohan and her mom?

Okay, maybe it's not in Rory's character to get into substance abuse and partying, so Lorelai is off the hook there. But what happens when romance comes to Stars Hollow? Many a friendship has fallen apart when a guy becomes "the most important one." And because the bond between Lorelai and Rory is so ultra-close, when sex and romance enter the picture, their relationship seems particularly vulnerable.

The first "intruder" is Max.

Max is a teacher at Rory's school. Lorelai has an affair with him. They're even gonna get married. Will this upset the balance?

Max tries to fit in to the Gilmore household. He cooks them food on pots they didn't know they owned. He watches *Billy Jack* with them, tolerating how they quote favorite lines, give away the plot, and shush him when he asks questions. But he's inevitably the odd man out. You really know this relationship is not going to work the night he sleeps over for the first time. Lorelai gets up in the middle of the night and crawls into Rory's bed. She says it's weird because she has a "boy in her room."

> LORELAI: Wake up, wake up. We've not properly talked about this.
> RORY: About what?
> LORELAI: About having Max in the house. About the effect on you. Don't cover up anything. Let's get it all out in the open.
> RORY: I don't have anything to cover up. I like Max.
> LORELAI: I know you do, and that's good. But you know, once we are married, nothing will ever be the same again.
> RORY: I know.
> LORELAI: It won't just be the "me and you secret special clubhouse no boys allowed" thing anymore. ("Red Light on the Wedding Night," 2-3)

Okay, this is a little unsettling. Lorelai can't deal with having Max in the house. She can't allow him to come between her and her Rory. Young, hip mom is freaking out about getting married. When it comes time for her to have what we might call a "mature relationship," this mom and daughter best-friend bond actually keeps Lorelai from moving forward in her life.

And there is something else troublesome here. Even if it means having to rise above her own squeamishness, Rory has to take care of her mom's emotions. So there's a rather ironic role reversal going on: the best-friend daughter has to mother the mom.

As that same conversation continues, Rory reassures Lorelai that it's okay to be in a relationship.

> RORY: Aren't you happy?
> LORELAI: Yes. I'm happy.

RORY: Well, then it'll be fine. You'll get used to it, having Max there.
LORELAI: I know. You're right. I will. I will get used to it. (Lorelai
    closes her eyes.)
RORY: Mom.
LORELAI: Hm?
RORY: You're falling asleep.
LORELAI: So?
RORY: You need to be a big girl and go to your own room.

As a wannabe hip if not young mom, I can attest to the fact that
there is something very appealing about imagining that your daughter is more together than you are—that she has miraculously (or,
well, thanks to your best-friend mothering) developed into a human
being who can take care of herself, is not too troublesome, and is
pretty much together when it comes to love, life, and getting into college. But still, we all know the mom is supposed to be the grown-up
and the daughter gets to be the one with the problems. Lorelai and
Rory are paying a price for all this chumminess.

Lorelai proceeds to dump Max. And she avoids commitment for
the next few seasons of the show. Yes, Christopher buzzes in and out
of the picture and Luke is always around—at just the right distance.
His diner provides a "kitchen away from home," with the man-figure
tantalizingly present yet peripheral.

But the center of her world is Rory.

And the center of Rory's world is Lorelai.

It cannot, however, stay like this forever. Rory needs to become
independent from mom and experience intimate relationships with
other people. And Lorelai, no matter how painful the prospect, needs
to let her.

When fifteen-year-old Rory is dating her first boyfriend, Dean,
there is a hint of the trouble to come. Lorelai has to deal with the
fact that her daughter is preoccupied with someone who is not Lorelai. Dean is sweet and polite and works part-time in the town grocery
store. He helps refill their water cooler and even presents Rory with
a car that he's restored. But Dean isn't too much of a threat because
he's, well, kinda boring. He isn't dynamic enough to supplant mom
and never presents any kind of challenge to the status quo.

But then Jess comes to town.

Jess is Luke Danes's troubled nephew. He lies, steals things, and—

even more worrisome—reads a lot, is really good at banter, and is really, *really* good at kissing. (So good, the actor became Alexis Bledel's real boyfriend off the show.)

It's enough to make a best-friend mom downright schizophrenic. When Jess and Rory get into a car accident, Lorelai goes ballistic and makes it quite clear she doesn't want her daughter to associate with the guy. Lorelai is in full "mom" mode, and does not resemble a best friend in the least. Her worst fear seems to be that Rory might lose her virginity to Jess.

One weird moment happens when Lorelai is eavesdropping on Paris and Rory. When Lorelai hears that Paris has had sex and Rory, now seventeen, is still a virgin, she smugly says to herself, "I've got the good kid" ("The Big One," 3-16).

Is this the same woman who had a baby out of wedlock when she was sixteen? Perhaps the prospect of your own daughter having sex makes even the youngest, hippest mom channel Newt Gingrich, Anthony Comstock, and Andrea Dworkin. I do know I never hesitate to remind my daughter that she should always use condoms, even if she's on the pill, because she could still get syphilis, gonorrhea, herpes, AIDS....It's almost as if I want these frightening diseases to scare her into celibacy, even though I of course want her to enjoy her sexuality.

Before too long, Rory seems to have put "losing virginity" on her to-do list. And she tells Lorelai her intentions.

RORY: Nothing's happened yet, but...it might. Maybe.
LORELAI: Maybe?
RORY: Maybe...with Jess.
LORELAI: Hm, with Jess.
RORY: You still want me to tell you everything, right?
LORELAI: Yeah. Uh, no. Well—
RORY: Which is it?
LORELAI: We're doing this now.
RORY: Yes. Which is it?
LORELAI: I don't know.
RORY: You'll let me know?
LORELAI: Yeah.
RORY: Was that, yeah, you'll let me know, or yeah, that's your answer, you wanna know?
LORELAI: I guess, I want to know, yes, and now, sure.

The language is especially awkward. No clever repartee here. When it comes to sex, the Gilmore Girls are as awkward as any mother and daughter.

RORY: Well, nothing's happened.
LORELAI: I heard.
RORY: But it might.
LORELAI: Okay. Could you tell me before it does?
RORY: Right before, or—
LORELAI: No, just…just before.
RORY: Okay. ("Swan Song," 3-14)

Lorelai's request to be notified when her daughter is going to have sex seems like a desperate attempt to maintain the status quo: we are best friends; we tell each other everything. She puts her arm around Rory, and Rory puts her arm around Lorelai, and they begin to eat. And they both look very uncomfortable.

Rory's first sexual experience is not destined to be with Jess, though. He leaves town, and Rory goes off to Yale. She doesn't get serious with any guy her first year of college. And then she ends up having sex, surprisingly, with the now-married Dean. And she does not consult with Lorelai first.

When Lorelai discovers the truth, she does not take it well. She insults Rory in a very Emilyesque way. "I didn't raise you to be like this. I didn't raise you to be the kind of girl who sleeps with someone else's husband" ("Raincoats and Recipes," 4-22). In fact, she reduces Rory to tears. The season ends with the two fighting and then picks up again in the same place in the fall.

LORELAI: I give up. It's your life. Do what you want.
RORY: Thank you.
LORELAI: You're nineteen. You know what you're doing.
RORY: I do know what I'm doing.
LORELAI: So you don't want to talk. We won't talk.
RORY: Good.
LORELAI: I wasn't thinking we had to talk like mom and kid. I thought we could talk as friends, but hey, forget it.
RORY: I will. ("Say Goodbye to Daisy Miller," 5-1)

Now that Rory has an active sex life, it's just not the same between mother and daughter. I think it would be safe to say that for most mothers and daughters—even today's most chummy ones—this is a point in the relationship where there is a drawing back. There's just something so intrinsically icky (for lack of a better word) about it. Few daughters want to confess to mom about doing the dirty. And even the coolest Boomer mom isn't too keen on hearing the details of her daughter's sex life. You could argue that this is a time when communication is more important than ever. (Yes, I am trying to sound mature, here.) But hey, who wants to discuss topics like, *Where did you get those cherry-flavored ribbed condoms I found in your sock drawer?*

I don't know exactly when my daughter lost her virginity. For a long time, I assumed this was something I would most certainly know. I thought, when the time came, I'd be too curious not to ask. But the more she was doing, the more I shied away from the specifics. It just didn't seem like my business. My comments became more cautionary, hers more dismissive.

> ME: Please just make sure that you only have sex with someone when you're in a loving, happy relationship.
> HER: Mom, you've been watching too much *Gilmore Girls*.

In any case, the relationship with Dean does not last long. Rory is settling in at Yale; basically, he has no chance. Rory becomes preoccupied with the ultimate threat to the mom and daughter best-friend bond: Logan Huntzberger.

Logan, a student at Yale, is the son of an extremely wealthy newspaperman. His family is exemplary of everything Lorelai despises about the social sphere in which her parents orbit.

Rory is incredibly attracted to him.

And she's really afraid to let her mother know this.

Lorelai is quite clear on how she feels about "vapid, selfish" rich people like the Huntzbergers: "These people live in a universe where they feel entitled to get what they want, when they want it, and they don't care who's in their way. I hate that world" ("Wedding Bell Blues," 5-13).

The romance blossoms anyway, and Rory keeps that pretty quiet.

But then Logan's father undercuts Rory's abilities as a journalist. In the grips of an extreme meltdown, Rory proceeds to steal a boat with Logan, get arrested, and drop out of Yale.

Lorelai handles the theft and arrest parts of the meltdown with all the coolness of a young, hip mom. But she can't stand the idea that Rory is giving up her Ivy League education—the opportunity that Lorelai never had. Mother and daughter have it out, and Lorelai blames Logan, saying everything has gone wrong since Rory started seeing him.

Rory—perhaps sensing that she's gonna need some distance from Lorelai over the summer to keep things going with Logan—moves in to her grandparents' pool house. She also joins the DAR (Daughters of the American Revolution) and basically becomes an Emily clone. It's the grandmother of all insults. The ultimate betrayal. Rory has defected. Gone over to the other side. Become one of them.

And, most traumatically for *Gilmore Girls* viewers across the nation, Rory stops speaking to Lorelai. They are incommunicado. Lorelai, who's been dating Luke for the past year, takes drastic action: she flat out proposes marriage. He says yes. So for awhile, the Gilmore Girls lead parallel and separate lives. It seems that they can only have serious relationships with men if they're not speaking to each other. It's distressing. The whole best-friend mom and daughter thing has totally backfired!

It's understandable that Lorelai would want to create a relationship that transcends the usual bond between a mother and daughter. After all, she grew up feeling constrained by her mother's needs and demands. In order to flourish, she had to rebel against Emily and everything she stood for. As Lorelai says: "My whole life, my whole existence, my essence, my being, my ability to be the sparkling creature who stands before you, all of this depends on the complete and total separation of my life from my mother's life" ("The Fundamental Things Apply," 4-5).

Her best-friend mom and daughter strategy is geared towards keeping that unhappy situation from repeating. As they say: you can't choose your relatives, but you can choose your friends. So, the "best-friend" bond proclaims: "I am with Rory because we chose to be together, not because we were randomly paired because of a practical joke by God."

Of course, Lorelai did not really choose Rory. The pregnancy was an accident, and in any case, a mother never knows who is going to come out. But Rory *was* "chosen" in the sense that most teenage girls would have had an abortion rather than keep the child. So on some level, Lorelai did choose to keep Rory. And then she raised her as a best friend, determined never to snuff the "sparkling creature" that is her own daughter.

Now, with Rory in the pool house dating Logan and organizing DAR functions, Lorelai has to stomach seeing her own daughter accepting her mother's values. Despite the fact that Lorelai has tried her darndest to ward against it, Rory is being as disappointing as she could be. She's rebelling against everything Lorelai stands for.

Lorelai has to make a decision. Refuse to accept Rory's relationship with Logan, which means she'll alienate Rory, which means she'll lose her just like Emily lost Lorelai. . . .

Or suck it up.

Can she? Is she willing to take a less important role in her daughter's life? Will she allow Rory to let Logan be the person she's closest to in the world?

This is the true job of the mother, isn't it? To step back when it's time to step back. To allow your child to make her own decisions— even if those decisions distress you to the core. My own daughter, I might mention, has recently done the unthinkable. She has up and moved out of the house. That's right, she's gone away to college. Her bedroom is empty! There are no clothes on the floor. No dirty dishes next to her computer. There aren't even any condoms in her sock drawer. How can she do this to me?

I, like Lorelai, realize I cannot control my daughter's decisions. If she wants to get an education, fine. I have a life. I have friends. I have *Gilmore Girls*. And if Rory wants to marry a vapid, selfish rich kid and spend the rest of her life throwing him dinner parties, so be it.

Lorelai sucks it up. She decides to try to like Logan, or at least get along with him, or at least keep herself from insulting him to his face.

Eventually, Emily has a falling out with Rory. No surprise there. Once grandma realizes Rory is having sex in the pool house, she threatens to ground her. Rory points out she's twenty-one and can't be grounded.

EMILY: You are becoming more and more like your mother with every passing day.

RORY: And you are becoming more like my mother's mother with every passing day. ("Let Me Hear Your Balalaikas Ringing Out," 6-8)

Rory ditches the pool house, moves in with Paris, and—not to worry—goes back to Yale. And she makes up with Lorelai. But it's different now. It feels different. The dynamic between mother and daughter has actually evolved.

This is especially apparent in the episode when Luke and Lorelai visit Rory and Logan at his father's vacation home on Martha's Vineyard. Rory seems all grown up: wears older, more sophisticated clothes, shows the house off as if she owns it, and chatters about planning a six week trip to Asia. (I'm presuming Logan would be paying for this? Or possibly Christopher.) She even cooks! Lorelai is in shock: "You're wearing an apron. You've not worn an apron since you saw *The Sound of Music* and you put one on so you'd look like Sister Maria, and you made a big crucifix out of Popsicle sticks" ("A Vineyard Valentine," 6-15).

Lorelai, engaged to distinctly working class Luke, feels like she's in a different social class from her daughter. She jokes that Rory has become too fabulous to hang out with her anymore. It really does feel like they've grown apart. They're each part of a couple that's doesn't include the other. They each have, at this point, more intimacy with the men in their lives. I might even submit that they are now mother and daughter first—and best friends second.

Why? Because Lorelai is allowing Rory to be different from her, different from what she wants her to be. In accepting this new Rory, she's doing what Emily can't. Lorelai is being a role model.

I suppose it's gratifying to see the Gilmore Girls growing and maturing and all that. But still, it's sad the way time marches on. I can't help but wonder: Will Rory ever move back to Stars Hollow? Will Lorelai ever marry or have another child? Will my daughter meet a vapid, selfish rich kid and make me feel like I'm in a lower social class? Thank god for DVDs and reruns. It feels good to relive those good old days—back when Lorelai was a best-friend mom first, and Rory was still a virgin.

Stephanie Lehmann is the author of the novels *Thoughts While Having Sex, Are You in the Mood?*, *The Art of Undressing*, and *You Could Do Better*, which is about a curator at the Museum of Television. Her plays have been produced Off-Off Broadway, and her essays have appeared on Salon.com. Originally from San Francisco, she now lives in Manhattan with her husband and son. Stephanie finds it hard to believe that she no longer lives with her daughter. Stephanie's mother says she'll get used to it, which may or may not be insulting. Stephanie's glad her daughter does come home from college to visit occasionally, and when she does, they enjoy drinking coffee and eating something with sugar in it and gabbing while watching TV. Stephanie does the same when she visits her mother. You can visit Stephanie at her Web site www.StephanieLehmann.com.

Charlotte Fullerton

In Defense of Emily Gilmore

EMILY (to Lorelai): You're muttering under your breath. Years of experience have taught me that when you do that, it's usually about me. ("There's the Rub," 2-16)

Emily Gilmore is the third Gilmore Girl and as such, Charlotte Fullerton argues, much maligned. A woman who's doing the best she can playing by the rules of her generation and her social class, Emily has much more in common with Lorelai than she or her daughter—or the viewers—may realize.

Hear ye, hear ye! Court is now in session!
The defense will now present its evidence in the case of the
Viewers vs. Emily Gilmore. All rise.

T'S NOT HARD to find ways to attack the eldest of the three Gilmore Girls. Emily is an easy target. If I had a nickel for every time I read a rant in an online fan forum about what a "bitca" Emily is, I'd have...a whole lot of nickels. She's a judgmental, overly critical, impossible-to-please, perfectionist, control-freak snob, who takes a sadistic pleasure in belittling those she considers beneath her in social standing, and particularly enjoys making her only offspring, Lorelai, miserable. And those are her good qualities! Okay, seriously. Taking pot shots at Emily Gilmore and her laundry list of faults may be cathartic, but it hardly scratches the surface of this complicated and therefore highly compelling character.

I do not intend to make excuses for Emily's often petty and vindictive behaviors and attitudes. But I do want to explore her *reasons*. Every real, live human being has his or her own personal internal logic that lies behind the choices he or she makes. Well-rounded, well-grounded, fictional characters like Emily Gilmore do as well. This is what engages us, convincing us to care about them as if they were more than just words on a page and actors on a stage. Now, whether a person's internal logic is ever obvious to those around them— or even to him- or herself—is entirely up for grabs. A blind spot for self-awareness can make for an interesting fictional character, if a frustrating acquaintance in real life. When actors ask, "What's my motivation?" it is a critically important question, not just the cliéd one-liner it's become. *Why* does this character think this way? *Why* does this character say the things she says and do the things she does? The Wicked Witch of the West is, well, just plain wicked and a witch…and presumably from the west. Emily Gilmore has a more complex character profile.

Exhibit A: The Definition of Success

Emily went to college at a time when earning an "MRS" degree (going to college mainly to find a husband) was considered a viable— even expected—pursuit, and not the post-feminism joke it is today. She is a graduate of Smith College, one of the five remaining, private, women's liberal arts colleges in the northeast still known as the Seven Sisters, all now considered in some circles to be competitive with the Ivy League. Among notable real-life Smith alumnae are Barbara Bush, Nancy Reagan, and even feminist icon Gloria Steinem! So Grandma Gilmore is an educated, capable woman in her own right, as well as one who did very well for herself—or at least as expected—marrying young to trust fund Yalie Richard Gilmore. By today's standards, however, Emily would be considered to have completely squandered her potential, wasting her own talent, education, skills, and opportunities to play supportive wife to her high-achieving executive husband: a glorified secretary keeping track of their social engagements and busying herself arranging fundraisers and tea parties with various high-society charitable organizations in between hair appointments and managing their household staff with an iron fist. Imagine—if Emily had concentrated all that effort, energy, no-nonsense leadership, strict attention to detail, and my-way-or-the-highway attitude on something that actually *mattered* in the greater world instead of focusing it all on berating maids about the acceptable distance between candlesticks, what she could have done at the helm of a Fortune 500 company! Yet she resents her daughter Lorelai for having wasted *her* potential? Pot, meet kettle.

The thing is that, for the most part, Emily does consider herself to be a success story. And given the societal constraints during the time in which she grew up, she is. To Emily, the position in life she's carved out for herself by Richard's side is not only perfectly acceptable, but enviable. Why her own daughter—or anyone—wouldn't want to be in her (designer) shoes is a complete mystery to Emily. So naturally she was genuinely shocked and offended when, at Rory's twenty-first birthday party, her own husband gruffly blurted out that he wanted more for their intelligent and capable granddaughter than Emily's "frivolous" life among ladies who lunch ("Twenty-One is the Loneliest Number," 6-7). It was a good enough life for his wife, but not for his granddaughter? Richard backpedaled, of course: he honestly didn't intend it as an insult, but I can't help but wonder whether, were Emily and Richard twenty-one themselves nowadays, his aspirations for Rory would also apply to Emily. Impossible to say for sure. I do think that, somewhere deep down, Emily knows she could have run Richard's businesses at least as well as, if not better than, he has. But she would never even suggest something so—in her eyes—disrespectful to her husband, and certainly never in front of other people.

At some points, however, it clearly leaks through that, underneath it all, Emily is *not* entirely satisfied with her life. True, she resents it when others don't take her role seriously. But there are also times when Emily is openly impressed by and even downright jealous of her daughter, the capable, self-made businesswoman. The very few instances in the entire series that are a result of this jealousy— comparing herself to Lorelai and feeling the need to defend her own choices and lifestyle—are some of Grandma Gilmore's sharpest as well as most poignant moments, Lorelai is surprised and touched when Emily uncharacteristically compliments her dressmaking and parenting skills ("Rory's Dance," 1-9). In a later fleeting instance, Emily wistfully wonders why she and Lorelai can't have as close a mother-daughter relationship as Rory and Lorelai ("There's the Rub," 2-16). And, most outstandingly, when Lorelai and Rory are introducing Emily to the joys of the mall food court and Emily overhears Lorelai on the phone adeptly dealing with the Dragonfly Inn's start-up issues ("Scene in a Mall," 4-15). This last is a particularly banner moment in Lorelai and her mother's relationship, with Emily actually openly expressing pride in her daughter for the first and only time, even if that pride is tinged with envy and self-pity. And despite their friction, Lorelai was quick to leap to her mother's defense when Jason "Digger" Stiles callously canceled Emily's launch party for his and Richard's new business venture ("An Affair To Remember," 4-6) because she understands how much planning these society events means to her mother: that it is the only way Emily feels able to contribute in life. Seems Grandma Gilmore is a tragic character and she doesn't even know it! (If a tree falls in the forest on a tragic character but she doesn't consider herself tragic, is she?) It's hard not to wistfully wonder what Emily's life might have been like had she not chosen to marry Richard, in much the same way Emily herself laments her daughter's road not taken.

Lorelai, of course, vehemently feels that she narrowly escaped from a lifetime sentence in a gilded cage. But Emily adores the gild and dismisses the very notion of there being a cage! This is a fundamental difference between Emily and her daughter's conceptions of high-society life, on which they may never see eye-to-eye, and it explains a lot about their relationship. Where Lorelai sees confining, smothering, soul-crushing prison bars, Emily sees a perfectly comfortable life with far *more* freedoms (of opportunity) than Lorelai's, and honestly can't fathom where her daughter gets such melodramatic imagery.

In Emily's view, Lorelai *unnecessarily* deprived Rory during her childhood (prior to asking Richard and Emily to pay for Chilton in the pilot episode of the series) purely out of spite! That deprivation involved not only keeping Rory away from the obvious creature comforts of wealth but, for no reason other than Lorelai's own willfulness, also actively limiting Rory's chances of success by preventing her from taking advantage of every competitive edge at her disposal—i.e. those made available more readily (or even at all) only to families of a certain social standing. In Emily's eyes, pouting teenaged Lorelai was far less concerned with little Rory's long-term well-being than with her own pride, stubbornly working a low-paying, lower-class job, and hoarding young Rory away from her perfectly willing-and-able-to-help grandparents just to be contrary.

EMILY: (to Lorelai): Oh, you're so perfect and I was so horrible. I put you in good schools. I gave you the best of everything. I made sure you had the finest opportunities. And I am so tired of hearing about how you were suffocated and I was so controlling. Well, if I was so controlling, why couldn't I control you running around and getting pregnant and throwing your life away? ("Rory's Dance," 1-9)

It may appear that everything between Lorelai and Emily has to be on Emily's terms, but partly it seems that was because Lorelai inherited her mother's stubborn streak, so naturally would prefer everything to be on *her* own terms instead. She wants her mother to change/budge/see the error of her ways, but Lorelai herself rarely does. And the few times Lorelai has, it has only been with the most drama-queen-ing, woe-is-me-ing, eye-rolling theatrics: *allowing* her parents to lend her nearly a hundred thousand dollars for Rory's private high school education; *conceding* to Rory's decision to attend her grandfather's alma mater, Yale, instead of Harvard, on which Lorelai had always had her heart set for Rory. From Lorelai's histrionics, you'd think that by introducing her granddaughter to the perks of the upper class, Emily was trying to indoctrinate Rory into a mindless cult! (One of us.... One of us....) From Lorelai's point of view, that comparison's not far off.

This is why it was such a huge deal to Emily when Lorelai allowed Rory to participate in a coming out party with other debutantes at a "*Daughters* of the Daughters of the American Revolution" event ("Presenting Lorelai Gilmore," 2-6). Emily got to proudly show off her granddaughter to the approval of her society friends—whose opinion is, of course, a driving force in Emily's life—even while openly sighing that she never got to do the same for her own daughter. Again, what Lorelai classifies as a gratefully dodged bullet in her life, Emily tsk-tsks as a missed opportunity—for both of them, but more so for *Lorelai*. In Emily's view, she wanted more for her daughter in life than her daughter seemed to want for herself! From Lorelai's perspective, she was just yearning for things that her parents' world did not offer.

Exhibit B: Boston Brahmins

That world, the one Emily grew up in—the world she also *married up* in, if we can trust the judgment of Richard's mother—is marked by the values, attitude, and speech patterns, if not the actual accent and lineage, of the *Boston Brahmins*—a historical term introduced to many modern Americans for the first time during John Kerry's 2004 Presidential bid. It refers to a certain group of surnames, an elite clique comprised of a short list of WASP families descended from those who founded the city of Boston. Gilmore is not one of those names. The term Brahmin, however, has grown to generically encompass the whole New England prep school/Ivy League legacy crowd in general, "old money" families of certain breeding, and the specific characteristic hoity-toity accent made familiar to TV viewers by the likes of Charles Emerson Winchester III, Frasier Crane, Thurston Howell III, and Headmaster Charleston at Rory's fictional prep school, Chilton.

Richard's mother, Lorelai Gilmore the First, may not have been a true Brahmin, but she and the Gilmore set we've encountered obviously aspire to that echelon of New England society, mimicking many Brahmin traits. Richard was a Yale man, as was his father, and his father. We've been told a Gilmore came over on the Mayflower. Someone in Emily's family must have been documented as having fought in the American Revolution for her to belong to the Daughters of the American Revolution. And just as in many Brahmin families, Richard's mother even married a cousin with her same maiden name.

This particular New England caste system, and the invisible dividing lines of social strata, are vitally important to Emily. And many of Emily's most easily criticized tendencies are the result. Emily cannot, for instance, be bothered to learn the correct names of her hired help, and she proudly changes maids more often than she changes her mind. Emily even believes that all maids tell their children the combinations to their employers' safes so the children can grow up and rob them! So which very-bottom-of-the-social-ladder profession could possibly be the most horrifying for her own daughter to have ended up doing? As if it wasn't mortifying enough to Emily's sensibilities to have her sixteen-year-old daughter get pregnant, drop out of high school, refuse to get married, and run away from home with her baby, Lorelai ended up working as a menial servant: a maid! In Emily's insular little Brahmin-esque world, Lorelai's social freefall was an additional nail in her mother's humiliation coffin. How could her own daughter actively *choose* such a thing? Especially when—to Emily's mind—Lorelai had a world of other options available to her at the time.

Consider, too, Emily's reactions to Lorelai and Rory's choices of boyfriends in season five. She and Richard were beyond delighted when Rory first began dating fellow Yalie Logan Huntzberger, heir to an international newspaper fortune, and tripped all over themselves kowtowing to this young man a third their age but from a much higher social tier than their own. But when Luke and Lorelai started dating that same season, Emily's grand, sweeping complaint about Luke was that he was fundamentally not good enough for Lorelai. It didn't matter how well Luke treated Lorelai and her daughter, or that he owns his own small business (as well as the entire building it's in), or that he is financially stable enough to have had tens of thousands of dollars on hand to lend to Lorelai so she could open her own business. It was all immaterial to Emily, who is first and foremost blinded by the glare of Luke's bottom-feeder position in the social hierarchy. All she could see was that he was a "rustic" diner proprietor with no education, from a family that no one in Emily's world has ever heard of. He drank "nitwit juice" (beer) and drove a filthy, leaking pickup truck like a common laborer. Lorelai might as well have been dating the man who cleaned Emily's sewers.

When it began to look as if the elder Gilmores were going to have no choice but to accept Luke into their family, Richard coerced the naïve, blue-collar guy to his country club where he attempted to completely overhaul a blindsided Luke (by franchising his business, among other "improvements") into the kind of man the Gilmores and their friends might *possibly* be able to consider somewhat acceptable—or at least less of an embarrassment, if certainly never ideal ("You Jump, I Jump, Jack," 5-7). This was Richard's compromise. Emily was far less willing to let go of the class issue. Enter Rory's dad, stage left. For all of Christopher's many, many personal shortcomings (particularly as a deadbeat dad to Rory during her childhood), to Emily, Christopher Hayden at least came from an acceptable dating pool for Lorelai. Social standing trumps all else!

I'm not saying I agree at all with her method of assessing people's worth, only that we see where Emily's attitude comes from. It's not just random or unmotivated. It makes sense for her character. So the gestures she *did* eventually make toward acknowledging Luke were *huge* on Emily's part. She even flat out tells Luke he's "won"—not the warmest or fuzziest step, but a step nonetheless ("So...Good Talk," 5-16). And later, after she learned about Luke's daughter April, Emily voluntarily—if with forced false friendliness—engaged in a game of cards with a random child in Luke's diner, mistaking "it" for April ("The Real Paul Anka," 6-18). Backing down and allowing her family to potentially become cross-pollinated across social strata is a *tremendous* concession for Emily Gilmore. And though we may disapprove of her methods, we should give her credit for that.

Exhibit C: Acceptable Weakness

Despite (or maybe because of?) her education, breeding, and assumed worldliness, Emily actually has an extremely narrow, sheltered view of the world around her. Even in her many travels to Europe, she's only ever seen the filtered, five-star version. (Although if you were to ask her, she would undoubtedly insist she has seen everything that is worth seeing.) This kind of self-centeredness masquerading as self-assuredness is one of Emily's strongest—if double-edged—personality traits. If Emily says it is so, then it is so. No discussion. She only hears what she wants to hear...and she never wants to hear a dissenting opinion! You've almost got to kind of admire that level of narcissism. When Richard had a heart attack ("Forgiveness and Stuff," 1-10) and was lying in a hospital bed, brave-faced Emily adamantly informed her husband that she refused to allow him to die before she did. She insisted on going first! (Her frail husband, who knows his wife well, touchingly agreed to abide by Emily's new law of nature.) Also, whenever Emily feels slighted by Lorelai or Rory (e.g., "Rory's Birthday Parties" [1-6] where Emily is hurt by Rory's failure to appreciate or enjoy the extravagant party thrown by her grandparents), Emily's first instinct is to coldly shut the offender out: it's done, it's over, it never happened, moving on. She deals with things that upset her by never dealing with anything that upsets her. She simply wills them away! If something displeases Emily, she pretends it doesn't exist. She can't, however, dismiss the things that displease her about her *daughter* without dismissing Lorelai entirely, and that is a real source of tension, continually, for Emily.

Because of this, upon casual viewing, Grandma Gilmore can appear to be devoid of *any* emotions that don't fall into the passive-aggressive category. But scratch the surface ever so slightly and it's clear that Emily's feelings run plenty deep. She just seems to consider it pathetic and weak to reveal one's emotions to others. Her feelings are no one's business but her own; they are private. When Lorelai left home as a teenager with baby Rory, Emily (as Lorelai found out *decades* later from Richard) didn't get out of bed for a month! So for all her chilly façade, there is a feeling human being beneath it, even though she only ever allows the world infrequent glimpses. During her and Richard's separation in season five, all of Emily's conversations on the subject with Lorelai (and even Richard!) were clipped and practical. Only when she had a moment alone was she free to drop the façade, break down, and weep in private ("Emily Says Hello," 5-9).

Expressing soft emotions openly to anyone—and to Lorelai in particular—is akin to admitting defeat for Emily, and their mother-daughter relationship is nothing if not a competition in willfulness. When Emily finally met Mia, the woman who gave teenaged single mom Lorelai a home and a job at the Independence Inn, Emily, after giving Mia a bitter tongue-lashing for not having made Lorelai turn around and go home immediately, asked stiffly about any photographs Mia had from Rory's childhood—demonstrating a sense of regret at what she had missed that she would never have revealed to Lorelai ("The Ins and Outs of Inns," 2-8). Emily and Lorelai both have a history of hiding their private lives and true emotions from one another, usually opting instead for sarcasm, feigned innocence, martyrdom, digs, or the old Emily standby, the silent treatment. In season two, when Lorelai, fearing her mother's disapproval, shut Emily out of her wedding plans to Max, Emily was shocked, humiliated, and hurt to find out about her own daughter's pending marriage via a phone call from an oblivious Sookie extending an invitation to the bridal shower. Her response was to refuse to attend the ceremony by pretending to have other plans that day. In season six, Emily attempted to gain Lorelai's attention by relentlessly barraging her with anonymous deliveries of random items, then indignantly claimed to be simply clearing out storage space in the mansion. It's a game of pointedly indirect communication, and they both play equally well in their own ways. Like mother, like daughter.

Lorelai has, on occasion, managed to put her own recalcitrant attitude on hold, swallow her pride, and make genuine attempts to extend an olive branch to her even *more* stubborn and even *more* prideful mother, who—surprise, surprise—has actually responded by lowering her own emotional armor, if only the tiniest bit. After Rory's coming out party, Lorelai tentatively dropped by unannounced just to "hang out" in the garden with an at first suspicious, then guardedly receptive, Emily ("Presenting Lorelai Gilmore," 2-6). And after their mutual hurt-feelings-fest over Lorelai's secretive wedding plans with Max, Lorelai visits her mother at home, gingerly requesting her advice on which veil to wear, in a thinly veiled[1] attempt to finally include her mother in her wedding planning. In a touching, simple moment, Emily quietly suggested a tiara—like she wore at her own wedding ("Hammers And Veils," 2-2). And in season six, when Emily tried to mask her pain at her fight with a frustratingly defiant, Lorelai-like Rory by impulse-buying/time-sharing an airplane (because it's "frivolous" like everyone enjoys calling her anyway), Lorelai gently assured her distraught mother that Rory's recent stream of bad decisions were not Emily's fault, Emily hadn't lost her granddaughter the way she had lost her daughter as a teen, and that despite their contentious history, she hadn't lost Lorelai at all.

These quiet expressions of genuine love between this mother and daughter are few and far between in the series, which is why they resonate so achingly when they do occur. More often, to Emily, "love" is by obligation, not by choice—either a matter of family obligation or monetary debt, and ideally both. Even the Gilmores' series-long "Friday Night Dinner" tradition is just coerced payback masquerading as family togetherness. It's heartbreaking to hear Emily state so matter-of-factly (and at most points in the series, correctly) that the only way she and Richard can ever hope to be guaranteed to see their daughter and granddaughter is if there is a massive interest-free loan keeping them obligated to do so. Poor Emily is sure that people only love her for her checkbook. And it's not entirely untrue! So the first time Richard's mother visited, offering a quarter million dollar trust fund for Rory with immediate access, Emily planted seeds of

---

[1] Heh, couldn't resist!

doubt in Lorelai's mind by (not inaccurately) pointing out that with all that money at her disposal, sixteen-year-old Rory wouldn't need her mother anymore, and, "It's terrible not to be needed" ("The Third Lorelai," 1-18). For a supposed unfeeling, Machiavellian harpy, Emily is desperate for her daughter and granddaughter to need—if not want—her in their lives.

Verdict

The eldest Lorelai (affectionately called "Trix" by her son) also happened to be the mother-in-law from hell. Trix openly despised her daughter-in-law and got a sadistic kick out of making Emily scurry around in fruitless attempts to please her. She even wrote Richard a letter trying to talk him out of marrying Emily the night before their wedding! Perhaps Emily's keen awareness of what it's like to be considered not good enough goes a long way toward explaining her insistence on enforcing social rules on first Lorelai and later Rory: no one will ever think the same of her daughter and granddaughter, if Emily has anything to say about it.

Not un-ironically, early on Lorelai gave some useful advice to Emily about how to deal with Richard's mother's unending disapproval:

LORELAI: You need to develop a defense mechanism for dealing with Grandma.... Take me, for example.... I know there are many things in my life you don't approve of... like this couch.

EMILY: Well, this couch is terrible.

LORELAI: Okay. Good. You think the couch is terrible. Now, at one point in my life, you saying a couch, that I carefully picked out and had to pay off over eight months, is terrible might have hurt my feelings. But not any more.... Because one day I decided instead of being hurt and upset by your disapproval, I'm going to be amused. I'm going to find it funny. I'm even going to take a little bit of pleasure in it.

EMILY: You take pleasure in my disapproval?

LORELAI: I encourage it sometimes just for a laugh. ("That'll Do, Pig," 3-10)

Clearly Lorelai often says and does things just to elicit a reaction—any reaction—out of her mother. Some people (even Lorelai herself!)

would suggest that Lorelai's primary motivation in every single decision in crafting her life, large or small, may very well childishly have been just to establish herself in direct opposition to her parents, and Emily in particular ("Lorelai's First Cotillion," 7-3). This relentless angling for Emily's negative attention—likely thanks to rarely receiving any positive attention—has apparently stunted Lorelai's growth as an adult. She may *seem* to have released herself at an early age from her mother's influence, but as long as she allows Emily's opinion of her to be the end-all, be-all of her decision-making process, Lorelai will always be an emotional child. Is it Emily's fault that her nearly middle-aged daughter continues to place such a high value on her opinion, even while proclaiming not to care? No one's arguing that Emily deserved a Mother of the Year award for Lorelai's childhood. But that was a long, long time ago. Lorelai has made all her own decisions since she first cut Emily and Richard out of her life at seventeen. What could Emily possibly do now that would make her daughter stop revolving around her, whether she's physically present or not?

I've long thought the most powerful way, dramatically speaking, for this series to end would be with Emily's death. Only then would Lorelai be forced to truly grow up. She'd have no more excuses for not allowing herself to fully become her own person separate from her mother.

Until then, Emily Gilmore remains a powerful force in her daughter's life and in this series. She is one of the unspoken *Gilmore Girls* of the title: a fascinatingly complex, layered fictional human being with her own reality, reasoning, character flaws, motivations, and emotional truths. Grandma Gilmore *could* have charged out of the gate a one-note, Wicked Witch of the West caricature and stayed that way. But thanks to the fortuitous combination of layered writing and actress Kelly Bishop's subtle portrayals, instead a formidable, flawed, and ultimately believable character has come to life.

The defense rests.[2]

---

[2] After spending any length of time with Emily Gilmore, wouldn't you need to?

Charlotte Fullerton grew up in New England with the same school uniform, hairstyle, and academic attitude as Rory, but left her own version of Stars Hollow behind for Los Angeles to attend the University of Southern California's School of Cinema-Television. Currently, Charlotte is a busy freelance writer of children's books, pop culture magazines, and some of your kids' favorite animated TV shows. Still, she is perhaps best known as one of the creators of the fan-favorite *Star Wars* short film, *Troops*. Whenever Charlotte gets homesick, she has lunch on the Warner Brothers' lot and walks around the *Gilmore Girls'* exteriors decorated for fall or winter—which she doesn't have to rake or shovel.

Miellyn Fitzwater

My Three Dads

RICHARD: I haven't been in the mood to talk.
LORELAI: Well, we need to.
RICHARD: I felt like reading.
LORELAI: Why are you doing this, Dad?
RICHARD: Well, reading is good for you. You learn things.
("Afterboom," 4-19)

While much has been written about the women of *Gilmore Girls*, the men have gotten short shrift, particular the fathers. Miellyn Fitzwater talks about why, analyzing Rory's three father figures. Put them all together, she concludes, and they spell "Father," but Lorelai spells "Mom" just fine all by herself.

W HO'S YOUR DADDY? The guy who cheers you on at your soccer games? The man who helps you with your homework? Your mother's boyfriend? The sperm donor? TV doesn't have just one answer anymore.

No way does Rory Gilmore need a dad to make her single parent home any sweeter. She's got a kick-ass mom who can be her best friend one minute, watching classic movies and eating junk food, and seamlessly switching to the super cool, understanding, and supportive parent the next. At first glance this family unit of two is a perfect little insulated world. But upon closer inspection, Rory actually has three major and influential father figures in her life, each one appealing to a different aspect of her character. In fact, they take up so much room in her life that her existence is not that different than it would have been if she had grown up with a father in the home.

I have thought long and hard, done many Internet searches, and endlessly harassed my boyfriend and co-workers to help me think of appropriate pop culture analogies for each of these men and their unique roles. I am now convinced they do not exist. These three fathers do not fill any typical television or movie father roles. They do not provide comic relief. They do not own cars that the child covets. They do not keep beer in the fridge that the child and her friends steal and get drunk on. In fact, most television and movie archetypes have more to do with fathers and sons than fathers and daughters. This is part of why *Gilmore Girls* is such a popular series. It appeals to a segment of the population that is not often represented on television. In filling that role, the writers take care to have characters that are realistic—in that special, hyper-realized kind of way that television demands. And it works because it has a ring of truth to it.

Rory has three main men in her life. The first is her mother's friend, owner of the local diner, Luke Danes. He is the gruff, somewhat distant yet caring male figure, the only one who saw her every day as she grew up and the one who has been quietly in love with her mom for years. The second is her grandfather, Richard Gilmore. He is the intellectual role model who expects only the best out of Rory and usually gets it, the man who has laid all of the hopes he had for his own daughter onto his granddaughter, the next generation of Gilmores. Finally, she has her natural father, Christopher Hayden. He is the fantasy, the absentee father who is always just out of grasp—idealized, yet majorly flawed, appearing only sporadically to spend time with her.

Rory's interaction with these men, in contrast to their interaction with Lorelai, brings an interesting dimension to the series. Rory and Lorelai can be seen as the same person separated by time/age and set on two different paths, with the fork in their road going Ivy League versus having a teen pregnancy. Lorelai made sure that she raised Rory to be the "new and improved" version of herself, teaching Rory everything she had to learn the hard way. And these differences between them are more sharply drawn because of the way these three men react to and interact with them.

Interestingly enough, though the series is very pro-female, none of the men challenge that. In my opinion, this makes the show every bit as pro-male. Each of Rory's enlightened father figures believes in her intelligence and in her ability to handle any situation, academic or otherwise. Her gender never comes under discussion. They actually have relatively progressive expectations for her, preferring that she continue her education and then pursue a career. They each want the best for her and for their relationship with her. Any mistakes they make appear to be made with the best of intentions.

So, on to the first father. The one who has been in Rory's life the longest and the most dependably... Luke Danes.

Luke is the one who has seen Rory daily for almost half her life. Rory gets some of her sense of stability from Luke. He is always there for her and for Lorelai. Though he is a constant source of support, he is somewhat remote at the same time. He is the father who loves you but maybe doesn't say it with words—it's the kind of love that becomes evident when something bad happens. These are the times when Luke is instantly protective, always coming down on Rory's side. His affection for her is always clear, but it became particularly obvious when Rory got back together with Dean. He never liked Dean, and after Rory slept with "married Dean" and then tried to have a relationship with him, Luke couldn't deal with it. Luke viewed Dean as a threat to Rory's purity, to her girlhood. Luke continually clings to the image of Rory as a little girl—in his mind she will always be twelve years old. He is often surprised when she acts like an adult, particularly when she curses or interacts with a male suitor in front of him.

Luke even feels like he has more of a right to be Rory's protector than her natural father, Christopher, does. These feelings came out during the reception for the renewal of Richard and Emily's wedding vows. When Lorelai, closely followed by Christopher and Luke, discovered Rory and Logan making out in a back room, Christopher and Luke both reacted as though they were the one man who had the right to tell Logan to back off. They went on to argue about it, during which Luke accused Christopher of not having been around when Rory needed a father growing up; that, coupled with the fact that Luke and Lorelai were together, made Luke feel like he had more of a right to claim Rory than Christopher did.

Perhaps the biggest gesture that demonstrated Luke's feelings about Rory was when he gave her the pearl necklace that belonged to his mother. He did so casually, claiming that he brought a gift in case

Lorelai had forgotten (which obviously would never be the case—feud or no feud, Lorelai would bring her daughter a present for her birthday). This is an heirloom of Luke's. The viewer knows how important family possessions are to him, since he made such a fuss over his father's boat and where it should be stored; he also showed the same attachment toward and care for his grandmother's bedroom set. The bedroom set is clearly something he specially values, and he bestowed it on Lorelai after remodeling her house. This necklace, having belonged to his mother, must be of at least similar sentimental value, and he wanted Rory to have it. He thinks of Rory as family.

Not as important as the interaction between the father and daughter, but entirely significant, is the interaction between the father and mother. Luke has provided the only constant comfort for Rory's mother. Through all Lorelai's relationships, the run-ins with Christopher, the altercations with her parents, Luke has been there at the diner, ready to comfort Lorelai. He has always been prepared to drop everything to come to her aid. When Richard was hospitalized for his heart attack, Luke closed down the diner and took Lorelai to the hospital. In fact, he often closes the diner (something he very clearly would not do for anyone other than family) to do things for Lorelai. He helps her in situations he would never involve himself in otherwise, including helping move Rory to Yale. His support of Lorelai grew after they became engaged. Lorelai even said later that she was sure she wanted to marry Luke the moment she truly realized how much he cared about Rory. Lorelai and Rory's feud was still going on when Luke and Lorelai got engaged, and Luke was the one who told Rory the news about the engagement. He talked to her several times before she ever called Lorelai directly. When Lorelai lit into Luke for telling Rory any information about her life, Luke responded that he felt caught between the two of them. His loyalties, clearly, are almost equally divided.

Then on to the one who controls her trust fund, the man who at times helps make her current life possible, the shrewd businessman who wants to pass on everything he knows... her grandfather and teacher, Richard Gilmore.

Rory got some of her value for education from Richard. They delight in what they have in common, in their interest in current events and politics, and their passion for books and learning. Almost their entire relationship is based around their intellectual connection, so much so that Richard can list her accomplishments off the top of his head (but might be hard-pressed to name her favorite food). When Richard had his heart attack, Rory sat with him and read to him from the *Wall Street Journal* and the *Financial Times*. Subsequently, Richard was the one who influenced Rory to go to Yale. Richard went to Yale and wanted Rory to follow in his footsteps, to become like him. He didn't just suggest this. He started campaigning for it, even tricking Rory into touring the campus, making it clear how important it was to him. And Rory was Richard's choice of "best man" when he renewed his wedding vows with Emily.

Richard looks to Rory to be the daughter he feels he was robbed of when Lorelai left home. It appears that he thinks it wasn't just the pregnancy that took Lorelai away from him; it was her refusal to marry Christopher. In Richard's mind, Christopher could have stayed in Hartford, married Lorelai, and joined Richard's firm. It was Lorelai who made the decision to go against the plan, sending Christopher off to pursue his education and then herself leaving shortly after, going to Stars Hollow on her own and depriving him also of the chance to watch his granddaughter grow up. This was Lorelai's greatest rejection of her father, and he has never really gotten over it or forgiven her for it.

Richard became Rory's father in an even more real sense when she moved in after dropping out of Yale. With Rory living at his house, he began to concern himself with the everyday details of her life. Through a series of encounters with Logan, including a conversation that Logan mistook as being about his "intentions" toward Rory, Richard began to inquire deeper into Rory's personal life. It makes sense that Logan took this so seriously. Since Logan had almost no contact with Christopher or Luke, as far as he was concerned, Richard was the father he had to worry about and avoid. When Richard became aware that Logan and Rory thought he was asking if they were to be married, he was surprised. It never occurred to him that Rory would consider marrying Logan. Richard was certainly opposed to the idea, regardless of the fact that he and Emily had married at that age. To Richard, it was different because Rory had things to do—

things that, apparently, Emily did not at the same point in her life. It is clear that he has bigger expectations for Rory than he does for Lorelai or Emily, a fact that Emily found insulting. As Richard learned more about Rory's day-to-day life, he came to fear for her virginity. As he refused to be robbed of another daughter, he enlisted Emily to take measures to interfere. Later, Emily even accidentally referred to Richard as Rory's father in trying to ground her, threatening her with the typical "When your father gets home" ("Let Your Balalaikas Ringing Out," 6-8).

He also was finally swayed to Lorelai's side and played a large part in driving Rory back towards Yale. When confronted by Mitchum Huntzberger, he finally learned the truth about Rory leaving Huntzberger's paper and, shortly after, Yale. Mitchum told Richard that Rory wasn't talented and that he had told Rory his opinion as well. Richard was shocked that Mitchum would "crush" Rory's ambitions. Richard felt, as any good father would feel, that Mitchum was crazy to think that Rory wasn't talented. The idea, and Mitchum's insult, angered him and finally galvanized him into action. He went by himself to talk to Lorelai about getting Rory back into Yale, offering to team up with Lorelai in a pseudo-parental unit.

Lorelai, however, consistently rejects Richard's attempts to be a father to Rory. The relationship between Lorelai and Richard is so damaged, and has been for so long, that she cannot accept his actions at face value. She is always looking for an ulterior motive that involves him using Rory to get back at her. In her mind, nothing comes free from Richard Gilmore. This distrust often interferes with Rory's relationship with him, putting Rory in the middle. They function almost as if Lorelai and Richard were Rory's divorced parents.

And then onto the natural father, out of reach, somewhat out of touch—the absentee father who loves her and wants to be a better father than he is but doesn't know how, passing through town only sporadically . . . Christopher Hayden.

Christopher flits in and out of Rory's life, having a relatively superficial relationship with her. He first appeared two-thirds of the way through the first season, randomly and casually dropping back into their lives. He'd never been to Stars Hollow; he'd clearly had little to do with Rory's life up to that point. He showed up claiming that he needed to tie up loose ends, indicating one of those loose ends was his relationship with Rory. From that point on, it was clear that he wanted to be around, and he always tried to make his brief appearances seamless, but was rarely successful.

Although he was the one who wanted to get married when Lorelai got pregnant (Lorelai sent him on his way to realize his career goals, which never really panned out), he doesn't seem to have made much of an effort to stay in close contact with Rory. This suggests that Lorelai's instincts were right: their relationship wouldn't have lasted. What attracted Lorelai to him as a teen—the irresponsible, sexy, bad boy persona—is what would have made it difficult for the adult Lorelai to stay with him and raise their child. She has been very careful to instill better values in Rory, while successfully managing not to force them on her. It's debatable how successful Lorelai was with this, however, seeing as the most serious of Rory's relationships are fraught with problems. She slept with Dean while he was married, she dated the emotionally unavailable Jess, and she moved in with Logan, who has gotten her into trouble numerous times (even getting her arrested), not to mention cheated on her. When he met Christopher they hit it off instantly, indicating that Logan is too similar to Christopher to be trusted.

When Rory's grandmother persuaded her to be a debutante in the second season, Rory was vexed once she discovered her father was supposed to present her at the ball. She asked Christopher if he would come, and he agreed, but she was not counting on him actually showing up. This was the first time we saw Christopher fully acting out traditional fatherly duties: helping to prepare for the ball, showing Dean how to tie a bowtie, and escorting Rory during the actual event.

Christopher's appearances in Stars Hollow tend to shake things up, always dredging up Lorelai's residual feelings for him. And Rory learns something very important from him, even though it's through his absence that she learns it. He teaches her the importance of responsibility and reliability, having suffered most of her life due to his lack of both.

When Christopher showed up once again seeming like he'd really changed this time, right before Sookie's wedding, he was newly sin-

gle. He and Lorelai connected. They decided to make a go of it, finally both on the same page about their relationship. When Christopher
told Rory, she was happy but warned him that this was something she
and her mom had been wanting for a long time, and that he should
be sure. Not long after, Christopher learned that his recent ex, Sherry, was pregnant, and he immediately knew that he had to be there
for that baby. He had missed everything with Rory, and he said that
he never forgave himself. He definitely didn't want to repeat that mistake. It's so John Lennon and the Julian versus Sean saga that it's frustrating to watch. He doesn't even say goodbye to Rory, bailing in the
middle of the wedding and leaving a farewell message with Lorelai.

His relationship with Lorelai is far from Ward and June Cleaver's.
They are connected by such a strong sexual attraction and long-stand-
ing history, in addition to the fact that they have a child together that
they can never seem to get away from one another. At times, Rory
seems to only tolerate their relationship, becoming frustrated with
their on-again, off-again feelings. Rory so desperately wants a good relationship with her father, and she worries that the drama between her
mother and father will interfere with that. And though Christopher is
the least responsible of the three fathers, in Lorelai's eyes Christopher
can practically do no wrong when it comes to Rory. It could be their
history and their undying attraction that makes Lorelai give Christopher so much leeway. She has always been able to see his potential for
greatness, and maybe she thinks that if she believes in him completely,
he will finally one day fulfill her expectations.

In Christopher's defense, by the time he comes back into Rory's life
there isn't much of a space left for him to fill. This was underscored at
the reception for the renewal of Richard and Emily's wedding vows,
when he and Luke argued over who had the right to defend Rory's
honor. He felt so threatened by Luke's interest in Rory's well-being
that he put himself on the offensive, attacking Luke for caring. Christopher has always meant well; he's just had a lot of trouble doing
well. He is, for the most part, available to Rory when she needs him,
and, when given the opportunity, teams up with Lorelai to make sure
that Rory's on the right path. Also, he did fulfill the most important
role in Rory's existence: he fathered her.

Adding It All Up

Through their actions, each one of the men makes it clear that they consider Rory their daughter. To Luke, she's the daughter he never had (although he actually turns out to have a daughter, she showed up so long after Rory that she didn't take away from their relationship; it is interesting to note, too, that Luke's daughter turned out to be very much like Rory). To Richard, she's a second chance and a like-minded sponge for knowledge. To Christopher, she's the periodic obligation that he loves but doesn't feel particularly beholden to.

So how do they measure up, when compared to one another? The role of a dad isn't a simple one, but is often simplified in popular culture. So for the sake of this comparison I think we can boil it down to the three most often acknowledged aspects of fatherhood: time spent together, money contributed to the child, and emotional support offered.

Time

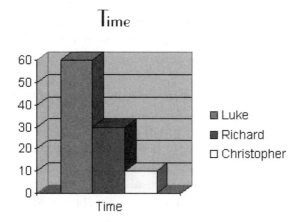

Luke has seen her the most, every day from when she was young until she left for college, if largely only in the diner, and continues to have regular contact. Score: 60 out of 100.

Richard took Rory in when she dropped out of Yale, lodging her in his pool house and therefore seeing her almost daily. Let's not forget the Friday night dinners that started when she was sixteen and, with relatively minor interruptions, have gone on through the present. Score: 30 out of 100.

Christopher could probably count on both hands the number of occasions he's spent with Rory. Score: 10 out of 100.

Money

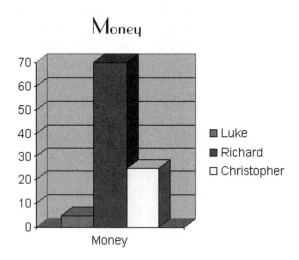

Richard paid for four years of Chilton, two years of Yale, a $40K renovation to the pool house, a fancy lawyer for her legal troubles, numerous parties, outfits, dinners, books, cash for her travels through Europe, and a car for her high school graduation. Plus, he was talking about springing for an astronomy building in her name at Yale. Score: 70 out of 100.

Christopher paid for one and a half years of Yale, bought her a compact OED, a Sidekick, and maybe coffee and food a few times. Score: 25 out of 100.

Luke has provided countless meals at the diner, sporadic household repairs, and the heirloom necklace that belonged to his mother. Score: 5 out of 100.

Emotional Support

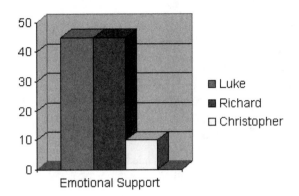

Emotional Support

Legend: Luke, Richard, Christopher

Luke is always there for Rory. He talks to her often, tries to help when her heart is broken, was there when she had the chicken pox, helped her move to college, talked to her when she wasn't speaking to her mom, and was quick to help when she was put in jail. Score: 50 out of 100.

Richard is the one she went to when she dropped out of Yale. He gave her a place to live and has made himself available to her if she ever needs anything. Score: 40 out of 100.

Christopher claims to be available, but bails on her at a few crucial points (such as the middle of Sookie's wedding, when he found out he was having another kid). He would like to believe if Rory really needed him, he would be there, but as much as his geographic location serves as a barrier, it's really his immaturity that continues to stand in the way. Score: 10 out of 100.

Totals

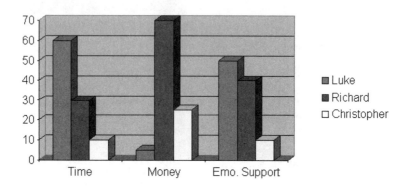

Richard comes out ahead with 140 out of 300, or fulfilling 47 percent of the fatherly duties. Luke is in second place with 115 out of 300, or 38 percent, and Christopher is trailing both of them at a mere 45 out of 300, or 15 percent. Although my emotional and sentimental favorite is Luke, Richard does measure up a little better as a father, at least by the numbers.

But this isn't a contest, and each of these men has something unique and valuable to bring to the table. Luke is the father of the heart, Richard is the father of the mind, and Christopher is the father of the body. One of them alone is not enough, but together they are Rory's dad. These men have ensured that Rory has received all the fatherly care and attention she deserves.

From the outset, people assume that *Gilmore Girls* is a series about women, but in fact it's just as much about men and the roles they play in women's lives. Each of these men fulfill their own niche, teaching Rory things that her mother cannot impart. And although it takes three of them to fill the role of father, while it takes just one woman to fill the role of mother, this is not because any one of them couldn't be a perfectly good father to her on his own, but rather because the situation prevents any of them from fully stepping into that role. Because of that, however, Rory really has the best "father" imaginable. Christopher has given her a sense of responsibility, Luke has shown her stability and honor, and Richard has imparted ambition and a love of education. This child of a single teenage mother actually has the strongest and most complete family unit on television, however non-traditional it may technically be.

Miellyn Fitzwater writes and produces television promos for TLC series, including *Miami Ink* and *What Not to Wear*. She has an essay included in the Random House anthology *Twentysomething Essays by Twentysomething Writers*. She has also penned and produced several independent short movies. She lives in Washington, D.C., with her very own "Luke" and their three plants. Miellyn not so secretly wants to be Amy Sherman-Palladino when she grows up.

Second Hamlet to the Right: Stars Hollow

Sara Morrison

Your Guide to the Real Stars Hollow Business World

TAYLOR: You would knock the crutch out from under Tiny Tim, wouldn't you?
LUKE: If he asked for a free cup of coffee, Gimpy's goin' down.
("They Shoot Gilmores, Don't They?" 3-7)

Ever wonder how the Black, White, and Read Bookstore stays in business? It's underwritten by fantasy, says Sara Morrison, who gives us a clear-eyed analysis of how the Stars Hollow businesses would fare in the real world. For starters, you can kiss Al's Pancake World good-bye.

F ROM THE HOSPITAL in a town that only has one stoplight to its geographically impossible distance from Hartford and New Haven, Stars Hollow has never claimed to have its feet firmly planted in reality. Rather, it thrives in a land of fiction, where Bridgeport (one of the scariest cities ever) has a clean, pleasant, and rather small seaside police station and rich society families live in Hartford (not too far behind Bridgeport on the "scariest cities ever" chart). As for the town itself, with its picturesque streets lined with beautiful brick buildings housing a variety of Mom-and-Pop businesses that somehow provide Lorelai and Rory with all those trendy, perfectly-fitting clothes, well, such places really only exist in our fantasies. And on the Warner Brothers backlot.

In this ideal world of bucolic perfection, life is easy for business owners. There are no franchise or chain stores to worry about when you're on a television show that can't use trademarks, so restaurants and grocery stores can flourish free from the specters of McDonald's and Stop & Shop. Their only problem, really, is that they have to hire Kirk over and over again despite his obvious inability to keep a job and his general weirdness, which tends to upset customers. One must wonder: How would Stars Hollow commerce do in the real world, where it would have to deal with real competition and a consumer base that needed it for its services and not solely to advance a storyline? As an amateur economist and former Connecticut small town resident myself, I feel I am uniquely qualified to answer this question.

Let's see how Stars Hollow commerce would do in the real world.

Dragonfly Inn

Let's start with the business run by one of the titular Gilmore Girls herself: Lorelai's Dragonfly Inn, purchased quite literally over its previous owner's dead body at the end of the third season and opened at the beginning of the fifth. Featured on the cover of *American Travel* magazine, the Dragonfly seems to be quite successful: it has a steady stream of customers and can afford to keep Michel employed despite his barely concealed contempt for everyone around him. In the real world, however, I'm not sure how well the Dragonfly would do. Stars Hollow doesn't seem to be much of a destination place, although it would certainly attract people looking to get away from the noise and dirt of the big city for a quiet weekend of antique shopping. I must also admit that my knowledge of successful small town inns and hotels isn't so great; the town I grew up in didn't have any inns or hotels, although it did have a string of trucker motels along the turnpike that could either be rented by the hour or the week. The Dragonfly Inn's a different kind of place. I do think it would succeed as a smaller bed and breakfast, but I don't know that the gourmet restaurant it houses would be as viable. Sorry, Sookie, but it's hard enough to find people willing to pay for four-star food in a big city, and Stars Hollow is a bit too remote to draw many outsiders there just for that. Even if it did, it surely couldn't attract enough to cover Sookie's high accident insurance premiums.

Chances of Survival: 25%

Luke's Diner

Luke's diner is a popular place in Stars Hollow, but much of that is a function of it being a place for characters to congregate and advance the plot. If a Friendly's moved into town, I don't know if Luke's could compete. His best chance would be to turn it into a twenty-four hour diner, thereby becoming the only place in town open after the bars close. Drunk people at three in the morning and old people at six in the morning tend to be the majority of the small-town diner's customer base. The fact that Luke's diner has been around for a while does figure well into its chances of success, as small-town people tend to be loyal creatures of habit and would therefore continue to patronize him instead of some fancy new franchise. Unless, of course, the fancy franchise had significantly better prices and better hours. Then again, Luke's diner has one thing the fancy franchises don't: local diner pancakes. Thick, fluffy, and cooked in an impossible-to-duplicate bouquet of greases from whatever was previously cooked on the griddle (most likely bacon, eggs, and a turkey melt), you just can't beat 'em. Luke's diner may not get much business during dinner hours, but would probably do enough business during breakfast to stay open.

Chances of Survival: 70%

Weston's Bakery

Better known as the place where Lorelai gets coffee when she's mad at Luke, this upscale place—and all the other coffee shops like it that have sprung up in Stars Hollow to enable Lorelai's coffee addiction—wouldn't stand a chance against Dunkin' Donuts. Even Lorelai would defect eventually, as their coffee is great. And mark my words, there *would* be a Dunkin' Donuts in that town. My town has managed to support at least two Dunkin' Donuts in its confines. Two Dunkin' Donuts, but no fancy coffee shops. We did have a bakery once, but, much like Fran's in Stars Hollow, it closed when its owner died. The building is still sitting there on a main drag, using up valuable real estate, and will probably remain there for years to come—until it's finally taken over by another Dunkin' Donuts.

Chances of Survival: 5%

Stars Hollow Music

Though this may seem like the kind of niche market that wouldn't do well in a small town, I think Stars Hollow Music would be one of its more profitable businesses. This is because it has a reliable and renewable pool of customers: school children. In my school, starting in fourth grade we were given an option to play an instrument in the school band or join the school chorus. No one wanted to join the school chorus. The local music store did big business every year renting out instruments to parents who wanted to encourage their children's musical enrichment but didn't want to shell out to buy an instrument unless they were sure of their kids' devotion to the craft (the time it took for this to happen varied depending on whether the instrument was a cheap flute or a pricey saxophone, but it was at least a few years). Cha-ching! Another draw to Stars Hollow Music is the fact that famous musician Carole King works there, although she can be very cranky at times and insists on going by the name Sophie.

Chances of Survival: 95%

Stars Hollow Books

Stars Hollow Books, on the other hand, is the type of niche market that would not do well. The problem with small town book stores is that they're never big enough to have the book you're looking for. With bigger chain bookstores having a much better selection, lower prices, and being within a relatively short driving distance, Stars Hollow Books probably wouldn't stand a chance. Not to mention competition from online retailers and the local library (Connecticut tends to fund its public libraries well, something I really miss now that I live in Los Angeles, which does not). There's also the fact that most small-town residents hate reading and wouldn't set foot in a bookstore unless it sold adult magazines. Stars Hollow Books might be able to survive if it switched to selling rare old books and jumped on the antiques bandwagon small Connecticut towns are generally known for, but that's probably its only chance.

Chances of Survival: 5%

Stars Hollow Video Store

This is a tricky one. Video stores in small towns tend to do very well, as small towns are boring and there's rarely much to do besides renting movies and video games. The town I grew up in once boasted several video stores, and they all flourished. Until, that is, Blockbuster moved to town. Blockbuster is open after eight o'clock and actually has new titles in stock as opposed to buying only three copies of the latest releases and renting them all out within minutes. All the residents who complained in letters to the local paper's editor that Blockbuster's presence would mar the "tree-lined boulevards" that never existed in the first place flocked to Blockbuster and never looked back. Of course, this was quickly followed by complaints about having to pay late fees and fond memories of the old Mom-and-Pop video store that used to forgive such transgressions until evil Blockbuster came to town and shut it down. I know this because I worked at that Blockbuster and had to listen to this all the freaking time.

Chances of Survival without Blockbuster: 99%
Chances of Survival with Blockbuster: 1%

Doose's Market

Taylor Doose's Market seems like a clean place that's big enough to have the selection and variety that would keep Stars Hollow residents loyal to it even if there was another, bigger grocery store nearby. Doose's will be especially successful if it has a good fresh bakery section, as townspeople tend not to trust bigger chains when it comes to baked goods and they won't be able to get anything from Weston's, since Weston's closed when Dunkin' Donuts came to town. Despite the fact that Doose's insists on selling those gross Red Vines when everyone knows that Twizzlers are the choice licorice of the East Coast and its pet food section is way too big, it shouldn't have any problems staying in business.

Chances of Survival: 80%

Taylor's Olde Fashioned Soda Shoppe

There's definitely a place for this kind of business in a small Connecticut town. While the cold winter months might be lean, the rest of the year should provide more than enough business. You could always tell when a Little League or a Youth Soccer game had just been played in my hometown, because the two local ice cream places would have lines of kids in grass-stained sports uniforms and their parents snaking out the door and into the parking lot. And in the summer months, Dairy Queen would have lines of almost Disney World proportions every single night. The other ice cream place was a small local chain that featured some of the best ice cream I have ever had. As long as Taylor provides his customers with good, inventive ice cream flavors (oh, how I miss the lemon pie ice cream of my hometown!) and/or standard vanilla and chocolate soft serve (with rainbow or chocolate shots, which is what we call sprinkles in Connecticut), he'll do just fine. That makes Taylor Doose two-for-two with his businesses. He may seem totally out of touch with the common man, but he's definitely got his pudgy, cardigan-clad finger on the pulse of small-town commerce.

Chances of Survival: 90%

The Town Troubadour

Technically, he isn't a business, but even so, the Town Troubadour would last approximately three seconds in a real small town before the local police (provided they could find the time in their busy schedule of setting up a speed trap on the same corner once a week) would rush in and haul him off to jail with the terrifying over-enthusiasm for their craft they usually reserve for those punk teenagers. I don't care how good the music may be—no one wants to hear it. The Town Wandering Weirdo is supposed to be as inconspicuous and out-of-the-way as possible, so as not to remind other townspeople that less fortunate people do exist and make them feel guilty about not helping. He could at least be helpful and earn some extra cash by going around with a stolen shopping cart collecting cans from the side of the road, like my town's version of the Wandering Weirdo, "Guy-With-One-Leg-Who-Always-Wears-A-Hard-Hat," did. If the Town

Troubadour could actually make it through a few songs without being physically assaulted, I doubt he'd make enough money to pursue Town Troubadouring as a full-time gig anyway. Small-town Connecticut people work hard for their money and are generally hesitant to part with it, especially for something as frivolous as live music. Maria Muldaur once swung into my town for a free concert and surprisingly few people showed up for that, so I doubt they'd contribute money to someone who didn't even have a "Midnight at the Oasis"-level hit. A real Town Troubadour probably wouldn't earn enough to buy a meal, let alone be asked to tour with Neil Young like the fictional one was.
Chances of Survival: 0%

Kim's Antiques

Despite the relative ugliness of its wares, Kim's Antiques should do pretty well, as antique stores are pretty much the only draw for remote small Connecticut towns and Kim's Antiques seems to be, oddly, the only one of its kind in Stars Hollow. The fact that Mrs. Kim isn't like the rest of the townspeople, what with her accent, religion, and eating habits, might cause some drop-off in sales, but she should get more than enough outside business to compensate for that. Hopefully, the confusing cluttered layout of her shop and her curt manner won't put them off. I don't know where in town she'll find decent vegan food, though.
Chances of Survival: 60%

Al's Pancake World

While residents might be able to get past the fact that Al's Pancake World no longer serves pancakes but still insists on being called "Al's Pancake World," they certainly won't be able to deal with its "international cuisine." Unless the international cuisine is Chinese, Italian, or possibly Polish, the townspeople will have no use for it and will find the exotic fare off-putting and even frightening. Oh, and let's also mention the fact that seafood from Al's Pancake World has been known to make both people and animals sick on multiple occasions. It only takes one outbreak of food poisoning to permanently close the doors of a small-town (or even a big-city) restaurant, so Al's would be doomed the second someone ordered those clams. Al would be better off running an International House of Pancakes than a Pancake-less House of International Cuisine.

Chances of Survival: 15%

Black, White, and Read Bookstore and Movie Theater

Yeah, right. The bookstore would suffer the same fate as its competitor, Stars Hollow Books, and I'm pretty sure the Stars Hollow Library has both a better quality film projector and a better selection of film prints than the "movie theater." You'd never find enough people interested in seeing an old movie, let alone an old movie missing one of the reels. You can only watch *Pippi Longstocking* so many times.

Chances of Survival: 0%

Gypsy's Garage

Though the sole red light in town may seem to belie this fact, Stars Hollow residents love to drive. So Gypsy's, as the only car repair shop in town, should be doing great business, especially considering the frequency with which residents wreck their cars by driving them into poles and buildings. As long as Gypsy stays fairly honest and charges a decent price, she'll be in business forever, even if a car dealership chooses to open in town—small towners don't trust those places and would much rather use the local mechanic whenever possible.

Chances of Survival: 85%

Miss Patty's Dance Studio

This might seem like a niche market that wouldn't do too well, but on the contrary, I think Miss Patty's would be very successful. I base this on growing up surrounded by female classmates who were all enrolled in various classes at the local dance studio, Caroline's. Man, Caroline must have been raking it in. And the good thing about running a small town dance studio is that you don't even need to be able to dance all that well; even the advanced classes are essentially for

beginners at this scale. And this is good, because Miss Patty's rotund form suggests that she doesn't do very much practicing in her off-hours, regardless of her oft-mentioned past Broadway glory.
Chances of Survival: 75%

Le Chat Club

A store devoted to cat supplies and cat-themed items that doesn't have the word "cat" in its name (yes, I know "chat" is French for "cat," but I'll guarantee you the vast majority of Stars Hollow residents and visitors do not) doesn't have much of a future, I'm afraid. I suppose Le Chat Club could survive for a while on the patronage of local cat owners Babette and Kirk, and people like Luke who don't know what to get people for gifts and settle on one of their tacky cat-shaped potholders, but even Babette couldn't possibly buy enough cat-related items to prolong such a narrow business's existence for too long. Maybe if Le Chat Club broadened its horizons and became a general pet store instead of being just devoted to cats it would have a better shot. Surely dog-lover Michel would shop there, so that's one new customer. A better plan, though, might be to actually become a clubhouse for people who like to chat. That would do amazingly well in this particular town.
Chances of Survival: 8%

Multi-Purpose Church Space

This isn't really a business either, but it is a central fixture of the town and should be mentioned. I find it incredibly ridiculous that a town with just under 10,000 people only has one building to use as a house of worship, and even that is shared by the several different religions. First of all, I'm amazed that there are several different religions in Stars Hollow. Second of all, I doubt they'd be able to work out a schedule where all of them could share the church space, or that their parishioners wouldn't find it a little sacrilegious. In fact, I'm pretty sure this is even *banned* by the Catholic religion, which understandably considers its holy buildings to be kind of sacred in that way. While I have doubts about the religious diversity of Stars Hollow, I don't doubt there are a considerable number of religious people in the town, and that would warrant the existence of several churches. I grew up in a town with far less religious diversity than Stars Hollow, and you couldn't swing a cat without hitting a church. I never had a peaceful Sunday morning there, eternally marred as it was by the sonic blast of church bells from one street over. And then there was the other Catholic church just up the street, which even boasted a convent at one time. So many churches. I'm not as confident about the synagogues, though. Stars Hollow claims to have a large enough Jewish population to have its own rabbi, but my town had twice as many people and I could count the number of Jews on one hand (we were the kids who looked slightly uncomfortable when we had to construct Christmas ornaments in public school art classes). Then again, my town shares its name with the capital of Germany, which might scare some Jews off (even though we took great pains to differentiate ourselves by pronouncing our town's name with the accent on the first syllable instead of the second), so maybe we were the exception and not the rule.

Chances of Survival: 3%

Antonioli's Restaurant

You can never go wrong when it comes to Italian food and Connecticut small towns. Especially if that Italian food is pizza. The only pizza place I remember going out of business in my town was a Pizza Hut, which sucked since it was the only pizza place that delivered. I guess their pizza just wasn't special enough to please the small-town palates when compared to the local places. Every time I visit home, I make sure to stop by the pizza place down the street, as it's greasy and delicious, the best pizza in existence, and I can't get it anywhere else. I think almost everyone feels that way about his or her hometown pizza parlor. So Antonioli's should do very well, even though the Antonioli family all have those rather insultingly stereotypical names: Luigi, Angelo, Gina, Maria, Guido, and someone who just goes by "Mama." Then again, I once worked at a pizza place run by a guy named Giuseppe and his son, who was also named Giuseppe. It happens.

Chances of Survival: 89%

Repertory Theatre

Did you know that Stars Hollow has a repertory theatre? It does, although you'd only know this if you've had the pleasure of seeing the set in person, as it never appears in the show itself—even though there have been a variety of events that could have been held there. This makes me think that it doesn't have much of a future, which is too bad since I'd love to see the townies all come out and put on a show there. It would be deliciously quirky and silly and everything a real Connecticut small town production probably wouldn't be. The closest my town got to anything like that was when the high school's annual musical was *Flower Drum Song*, a Rodgers and Hammerstein play with an entirely Chinese cast. My high school didn't have any students of Chinese heritage, so it ended up being more "disgustingly racist" than "charmingly quirky."
Chances of Survival: 1%

Stars Hollow Museum

Despite that fact that it only lasted one episode ("To Live and Let Diorama," 5-18), this place gets my vote for most successful business in the Real Stars Hollow. It might be my own personal bias talking, but that place was amazing. I would have gone every day. I'd have bought an annual membership entitling me to free admission and gift shop discounts. And I wouldn't have been the only one. Surely people would come from miles around to see this place. Even those disenfranchised punk teenagers would find something to love about the Stars Hollow museum—mainly, the fact that a cup of Miss Patty's Punch (main ingredient: grain alcohol) comes with every admission and is apparently given to all comers regardless of whether or not they're of legal drinking age. Plus, the diorama show mentions Jesus at the end, and small town Connecticut people love that guy.
Chances of Survival: 100%

And there you have it. I'm sure the Stars Hollowians would be sad to see some of their established local businesses go, but as soon as Wal-Mart opened nearby they'd be happy enough. (That Wal-Mart probably wouldn't open within the town itself as, if Stars Hollow is anything like my town, the residents will vote against opening a Wal-Mart in the city limits only to have two Wal-Marts open about 500 feet from either end of the town that everyone goes to anyway. Stars Hollow already has that one Wal-Mart nearby where Jess used to work, so it's due for a second one, preferably a Supercenter.). Plus, losing those less profitable businesses would give other enterprising townspeople a chance to open a few new businesses that Stars Hollow would surely enjoy. How about a package store (the Connecticut term for a liquor store)? Those always seem to do well, despite the fact that state law does not allow the sale of alcohol after nine o'clock or on Sundays. Thanks for that law, Puritans. A strip club would also be profitable, despite Taylor's best efforts to find something in the town's bylaws preventing a sexually oriented business from opening in town. Incidentally, a strip joint is also the kind of place where a real-life Lorelai would be likely to find herself employed, as a teenage single mom with no education. The newer, realer Stars Hollow would probably be a little seamier than the fictional one, as nothing sells better than alcohol and sex in a town full of people with nothing better to do. In the Family Friendly Programming Forum funding-free real world, even the prettiest tree-lined boulevards get dirty sometimes, and those charming brick buildings eventually fall to make room for a new pharmacy or grocery store. But Stars Hollow's quirky improbabilities are why we watch *Gilmore Girls*; they're what make its representation of perfect small-town life so special.

Former Connecticut small-town resident and amateur economist **Sara Morrison** does recaps of various television shows, including *Gilmore Girls*, at www.televisionwithoutpity.com. She resides in Los Angeles, where she gets way too many parking tickets. It's really not fair. This is her first publication unless you count "The Red Fox," a short story she wrote in first grade that was so good her elementary school had it bound and placed in their library. Sara hopes her hometown will allow her back in after this book comes out.

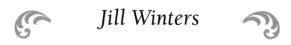

Jill Winters

Happiness Under Glass
The Truth about Lorelai
and Life in Stars Hollow

RORY: It's a Friday night. We should be out, I don't know, partying
with the homies.
LORELAI: Our Stars Hollow homies are all in bed by now.
("Keg! Max!" 3-19)

Jill Winters compares Stars Hollow to a snow globe, a picture perfect
place full of eternally content characters...and Lorelai Gilmore. Lorelai's problem is that while she's not sure she likes it in the snow globe,
she's not sure she wants out, either. Especially now that Rory's gone.

IT ALWAYS LOOKS LIKE OCTOBER in Stars Hollow, Connecticut. Picturesque New England town that it is, Stars Hollow seems
unfailingly temperate, colorful, and pretty. It's never cloudy. No
one's hair blows wildly in the wind; no one's umbrella flips inside
out during a torrential downpour. No one appears plagued by the
standard, oppressive humidity of a northeastern August. Populated
by people who are quirky but kind, Stars Hollow exists as a cozy, idyllic place, free of crime and malice, and full of simple charm.

So it's really no wonder that Lorelai Gilmore chose to raise her
daughter and build her life there. Or even that she would prefer it to
the affluent and more socially conscious world in which she grew up.

When Lorelai fled from her parents' home in Hartford, she was
only sixteen years old. Scared and pregnant, it was only natural that
she found sanctuary in Stars Hollow when the quaint Independence

Inn took her in and gave her a job. But long after she'd had her daughter, Rory, and become a self-sufficient woman, Lorelai still embraced Stars Hollow as her home, without question and with an implicit and unwavering allegiance.

Or so it would seem. She is an active member of the community. Her best friendships (with Luke and Sookie) and her professional ambitions (to run her own inn) both rest snugly inside the town. The diner that provides most of her meals and feeds her coffee addiction is only a walk away. (As is the pancake joint that serves stellar Chinese food.) Between lovable neighbors and local movie nights, Lorelai embraces Stars Hollow as unequivocally superior to the life that came before it.

But *if* that's the case—then why has happiness so often eluded her?

Over the course of the show, Lorelai has found herself in suffocating debt to her parents and gone from one failed relationship to the next. It would be tempting to blame her disappointments on the varying circumstances that accompanied them, but to do that would be to ignore the larger pattern of Lorelai's behavior—which reflects an acute ambivalence toward Stars Hollow.

Emily Junior

Despite Lorelai's vocal disdain for her parents and the wealthy trappings of their lifestyle, she is more like Emily and Richard Gilmore than she would ever admit. Especially Emily. In fact, while she may be wittier and more gregarious than her mother, Lorelai comports herself with an equivalent amount of self-importance. Lest we get seduced by the cult of personality, we need to set aside Lorelai's general affability and look at her through unfiltered glasses.

When we do, we see that she is vain. Sure, she might mock her mother for her preoccupation with "appearances," but conveniently, Lorelai herself is always stylishly put together. Her clothes are trendy. Her hair is curled. She usually wears makeup and she never repeats an outfit.

More importantly, she is arrogant. Where Emily is restrained, Lorelai is chatty—but either way, they are two sides of the same coin. Both are pushy and self-absorbed. Like Emily, Lorelai exudes a supreme sense of entitlement in nearly everything she does. Whether it was demanding that *she* be the one to choose the annual town square movie, or the time she showed up late and made herself the center of attention at Chilton's Parent Night, or the day she deliberately annoyed customers at Luke's diner so they would be uncomfortable and leave—thus freeing up the table where Lorelai preferred to sit—her sense of entitlement has never wavered. (And, like Emily, Lorelai has instilled it in her daughter.) In fact, in some cases, Lorelai is actually worse than her mother; while Emily is dogmatic in her devotion to social graces, Lorelai makes her endless, and often inappropriate, quips the center of every conversation she takes part in, even peripherally.

But Lorelai's resemblance to her mother goes beyond vanity. It's been nakedly apparent in the things she has wanted for Rory since the beginning of the series, which included admission to Chilton (an elite private high school), followed by a top-notch, Ivy League education. (And she may have paid a lot of lip service to the idea of "only Harvard" and "never Yale"—which was her father's alma mater—but Lorelai's loud protest against her "parents' world" was hollow at the core. As if sending Rory to Yale would be an admission that she embraced her parents' values, but sending her to *Harvard* was an act totally independent of them.)

So it was not a cruel quirk of fate that Lorelai ended up in debt to her parents. Rather, it was to be expected. Despite her endless derision for Emily's elitism, Lorelai clearly shared an admiration for the prestige and exclusiveness of institutions like Chilton, Harvard, and Yale. So much so that she was willing to let her parents have the satisfaction of financing both.

The Outsider Within

Despite Lorelai's tendency to reach outside of Stars Hollow in her aspirations for her daughter—and more often than not, reach *back* toward her roots—she remains sentimentally attached to the town. Comfortable. Determined not to leave. So every time she chose a boyfriend outside of the town, she was simply continuing on a recursive loop in which her romantic relationships were preordained to fail.

It was no bizarre accident that prior to Luke, all of Lorelai's romances were with men who lived a good thirty-minute drive away. Men who were more representative of her parents' social set than her own—men who would never and *could* never fit seamlessly into life in Stars Hollow. Not an accident, but rather a pathology—a telling one. Despite Lorelai's affection for Stars Hollow, she constructed her romantic life in sync with an underlying, yet persistent, desire to pull away from it.

First there was Max Medina, Rory's (pompous and unattractive) English teacher at Chilton (who had sloped shoulders and Eddie Munster's hairdo). Then there was Lorelai's on-again, off-again flame, Christopher Hayden, who is Rory's biological father. Interestingly, (arrested adolescent) Christopher is part of the same privileged Hartford set that Lorelai rejected—yet time and again, she has been drawn back to him. Next up, there was (nasal-voiced) Jason Stiles, who could not have been more ingrained in Lorelai's parents' world—he was Richard Gilmore's business partner! Nevertheless, Lorelai began a serious relationship with him, only to have it fall apart later when Jason threatened to sue Richard. On the surface, Lorelai's breakup with Jason was rooted in family loyalty, but I can't help but note that it came not long after Jason visited Stars Hollow, turned his nose up at Luke's diner, and took little interest in the town. Even regular-guy Alex Lesman, whom Lorelai dated briefly, was yet another outsider. Lorelai met him at a seminar she attended out of town, and their most significant date was spent in New York City.

So what does it all mean? So Lorelai happened to date men who lived outside of Stars Hollow. So she never considered dating anyone in town—a town with a population of 10,000—except for her longtime friend, Luke Danes. So that relationship fell apart, too—and she went running right back to Christopher. So what?

So, nothing just "happened." Rather, Lorelai, quite unconsciously, set up a conundrum. She firmly rooted herself in Stars Hollow—by psychologically ascribing it as home—then secured her future in the town by purchasing the Dragonfly Inn. And then she set about choosing boyfriends who were incompatible with her world. Boyfriends who, ultimately, would be unable to compete with the lure and comfort of Stars Hollow.

It was particularly symbolic when Max Medina sent Lorelai 1,000 daisies along with his marriage proposal (after she expressly told him that she would have liked 1,000 daisies along with his marriage proposal—so imaginative, that Max). Sure, she was touched by the gesture, but she clearly found more enjoyment in going around giving out the daisies to her neighbors than in thinking about marriage to Max.

To understand Lorelai's pattern, we need to understand what she has never articulated: her desire to be *both* an insider and an outsider in regards to Stars Hollow. From the series's nascence through today, Lorelai has wanted to be fully embraced by both worlds—Stars Hollow and the affluent Other, the world of her parents—yet to retain her position slightly outside of each. Where she can be a critical spectator. Where she can hold herself a little apart—and above. Purporting to identify with Stars Hollow, yet always making sure to have "a life" outside of it, Lorelai has never really seen her neighbors as her peers or considered them to be on her level—an attitude that is mirrored in her daughter, Rory.

What better demonstration of this push-pull dynamic than the regular town meetings? Lorelai and Rory have gone to every single one—and then spent the entire time mocking the proceedings. When Mayor Taylor Doose selected Rory as the town's poster girl, she railed against the honor. (Clearly she didn't consider it one.) With constant sarcasm, Lorelai and Rory often seem to be stopping just short of blatantly making fun of whomever they're talking to, whether it be Taylor, Kirk, Babette, Mrs. Kim, or any of the other Stars Hollow fixtures. (In fact, only their best friends, Sookie and Lane, have been consistently treated with respect.)

Like her mom, Rory has also sought romantic fulfillment in opposition to Stars Hollow. She broke up with Stars Hollow High basketball player Dean Forester in favor of (shorter, jerkier) "bad boy" Jess Marino, who made no secret of his loathing for Stars Hollow or his eagerness to leave. He was irresistible to Rory really because he articulated her own restlessness, which had only just begun.

When Jess left, Rory eventually backslid to Old Faithful—but ended up breaking Dean's heart again with her growing infatuation with (the perennially smug) Logan Huntzberger, a fellow Yale student whose extravagantly wealthy family had long been friends with Emily and Richard. There is a familiar pattern here—which is another way of saying, "like mother, like daughter."

But even if Rory's romantic interests could be satisfied in Stars Hollow, her goals and interests can not. Since high school she has aspired to be an investigative journalist. Before she'd turned twenty-one, she'd already been to Europe twice. In the latter seasons of the show, she'd even contemplated first a trip to Asia, then an extended jaunt to London.

Clearly Rory has striven beyond Stars Hollow in bigger, more dramatic ways than her mother, but...is the principal the same? Is there something missing in Stars Hollow? The same something that has kept Lorelai from committing fully to her life there—kept her just a little bit outside, looking in?

Which begs our original question: Why has happiness eluded her?

The Floating Jar

It would be easy to call Stars Hollow a "storybook world"—but it gets tricky when we begin to consider what story that book is telling. Apart from the Gilmores, Stars Hollow is its own narrative. Is it the story of small town New England? Or a deliberately implausible fiction? Is it constructed of events—or images? And where does individual "happiness" fit in?

When you consider Stars Hollow for what it is—pretty and self-contained—and when you consider that, aside from the Gilmores, the townspeople never seem to change much, Stars Hollow becomes like a scene inside a snow globe. Sure, there is activity among the locals. There are antics. People such as Kirk, Taylor, Babette, and Miss Patty swirl around, sometimes leisurely, sometimes frenetically—like little flakes in the globe, like objects in a floating jar—but they never really go anywhere. They don't change; they don't *grow*. And yet, they seem far happier than those who have tried to change their lives in a significant way while staying within the bubble of Stars Hollow, like Lane and Dean.

In fact, when the series began, Dean had just moved to Stars Hollow from Chicago. He was tall, cute, sweet, the ideal "catch" for any teenage girl. Yet, as the series progressed and Dean opted not to go to Southern Connecticut College but instead to get married and remain in Stars Hollow, he began rapidly losing his appeal.

It wasn't long before he was a bona fide town fixture, working at the same local grocery store that he had since high school and all but wearing his malaise like a drab parka. He might have ascribed feeling trapped to his annoying wife, Lindsay—and his affair with Rory to a natural result of that—but in reality, Dean's marriage was just a tangible thing to blame. He wasn't the cliché of "trapped in a bad marriage"; he was just trapped, period, again forcing us to confront the disturbing truth: Stars Hollow does not seem to be a place where one can evolve.

Happiness in Stars Hollow has always been a kind of stasis. A lack of drive to move forward and a contentment, instead, to float. To stay somewhat suspended—to stay the same. Like a snow globe, it's a beautiful scene and ideal only if a person does not strive beyond the glass.

Fittingly, most of the townspeople we have come to know don't really have any discernible goals. Even Sookie is among the contented snowflakes. True, she got married and had children over the course of the show, but the changes in her life were natural, comfortable extensions of her day-to-day routine. The man she married was her long-time friend. And her personal goals simply have not taken her beyond the glass.

Though she eventually partnered with Lorelai in buying the Dragonfly Inn, when the two had an opportunity to do some exciting traveling, Sookie enthusiastically encouraged Lorelai, telling her it would be a great thing for *her* to do. It was automatic; Sookie didn't even consider it as a possibility for herself. She simply had no drive for it, not even a remote interest in that level of change. But that absence of yearning is precisely what has made her happier than Lorelai throughout the series.

In my estimation, the happiest person in Stars Hollow has been the character who has most mirrored the town in terms of narrative expectation: Miss Patty, the overweight, unmarried dance teacher (who would've thought?). What have always defined Miss Patty are all the stories that came before. Like Stars Hollow, she came to us preset. Just as Stars Hollow is idealized, Patty's stories are romanticized. As a former dancer, singer, and stage actress, she has always existed for us as a compilation of memories—of a rich past that allows her contentment in the present. (In fact, *Gilmore Girls* even gave a nod to this in the episode featuring Patty's one-woman show, "Buckle Up, I'm Patty!")

But Lorelai has always been an innately restless work-in-progress. As such, she has kept herself at a slight distance from the town, avoiding a serious relationship within Stars Hollow—until Luke, which turned out to be just as suffocating a prospect as perhaps Lorelai always feared.

To followers of the show, Luke and Lorelai's long friendship-turned-courtship probably seemed fated. From the very beginning, there was an undercurrent of attraction between them. A near-flirtation in their daily banter. A special and resilient friendship. But when they finally got together as a couple...it fizzled. Their friendship suffered. Their communication failed at every turn. Even their chemistry was off. Resentment and awkwardness replaced their previously effortless rapport.

Granted, it didn't happen instantly, but over the course of two seasons. Their first big obstacle to overcome was Rory's dad, Christopher, whom Lorelai continued to spend time with while keeping it from Luke. As old habits die hard, so, apparently, did Lorelai's stirring to have a life all to herself out of Stars Hollow. The next set of problems began when Lorelai became engaged to Luke, thereby fully committing to him. Committing to a whole world inside a snow globe.

In spite of Luke's curmudgeonly disposition, he has always been more like Babette, Kirk, and Miss Patty than like Lorelai herself. Sure, he is amusing and sharp and not exactly a joiner—but he is also, unequivocally, a townie. He has never desired more than his day-to-day routine. He even had to be pressured and cajoled into putting a fresh coat of paint on his diner. No matter how grouchy he has been at the town meetings, townspeople have still remarked more than once that Luke would never leave Stars Hollow.

So where would that leave Lorelai—a woman who has kept just enough distance from the town's grasp to retain her autonomy? Once she committed to a life with Luke, how her world would shrink.

Season six of *Gilmore Girls* took hits from critics for its sluggish pace and for straying from its most basic tenets—namely, that Lorelai and Rory are more than mother and daughter, they are also best friends, and that while both are flippant, Lorelai is bold and Rory is reserved. But in season six, that changed. Normally studious Rory decided to steal a yacht, then leave Yale and bum around her grandparents' mansion. A totally uncharacteristic feud between her and Lorelai stretched on for episodes. Lorelai didn't fight to break the silence between them, but rather waited around, depressed, for it to end.

Meanwhile, Luke started pulling back. He'd learned that he had a daughter with an ex-girlfriend and then kept it from Lorelai. When he finally did tell her, he refused to let her meet the girl. The Lorelai whom viewers had come to know would never have accepted that. But this was a distinctly less spunky Lorelai, one with dwindling confidence and a whiny kind of insecurity. At first glance, it seemed she was acting out of character. But then—she'd never been in a situation like this. She'd never been in a state of relying *solely* on her life in Stars Hollow for her fulfillment. This was merely the result.

Interestingly, Lorelai wasn't the only character who changed with the circumstances. Rory seemed to compensate for her mother's reticence with an over-the-top flamboyance that ran counter to the *Gilmore* formula. Luke struggled with what amounted to the *inverse* of Lorelai's problem: Stars Hollow was swallowing her up, as the outside world was intruding in on him—on his comfortably closed-off world.

Or, to continue with the floating jar analogy, while one was stifled inside the glass, the other was panicking because the lid had been twisted off. Of course Luke felt affection for April, the daughter he never knew he had, but her existence still disrupted his life in a very unsettling way.

Unsurprisingly, by the end of the season, Luke and Lorelai had broken up. And even more unsurprisingly, Lorelai ran straight back to Christopher. Yet after spending the night with him, she lay awake with a pained look on her face. Again we had to wonder: What on earth does Lorelai want? What would make her truly happy? The answer has to lie somewhere between Emily and Rory, the two women closest to Lorelai—so close that they can't help but reveal her true nature.

Okay. So Lorelai shares her mother's frankness and her penchant for self-importance. At the same time, she feels a personal restlessness that Emily does not. Emily is urbane and well-traveled, *but* she has kept her personal world very small; she needs it to be small so that she can control it. Her friendships have more to do with social convenience than emotion. She keeps her husband, as well as her string of maids, on a rigid schedule of her own design. But for the fact that Lorelai can't stand her, Emily would be quite content.

Lorelai, on the other hand, craves something bigger. Like her daughter, Rory, she strives for something more than her immediate surroundings. Yet unlike Rory, she hasn't put a name to it. Her goals don't, by their nature, necessitate a life beyond Stars Hollow (as Rory's journalism career does).

Lorelai's "dreams" aren't grand or even clearly defined, but one thing seems certain: she is not prepared to swap goals for glass, no matter how pretty the snow globe. Looking at Stars Hollow as a narrative allows us to recognize its finite structure and that, as in any story, the textual landscape is what defines a "happy ending."

If happiness in Stars Hollow is a stasis, a kind of fluttering in suspension, and an absence, really, of longing and hoping far beyond the immediate, then Lorelai's best bet for happiness is not in the text itself, but perhaps in the white spaces. She is not trapped. Rather, in her defiance of Stars Hollow's constraints—and yet her refusal to relinquish her own important place in the town—she has, in effect, created her own niche. A place that exists not quite in Stars Hollow, but close enough. Close enough for Lorelai to enjoy a central role in the Stars Hollow "story." Undefined enough to give her freedom, power, possibility. And this seems to be the best position for a strong-willed, dynamic character like her. Because while the idyllic, almost surreal world of Stars Hollow may be the stuff of sleepy contentment—it's an implausible place for dreams.

A Phi Beta Kappa, summa cum laude graduate of Boston College with a degree in history, **Jill Winters** has taught Women's Studies as well as numerous workshops for aspiring writers. She is the author of five novels, including Lime Ricky, Just Peachy, Raspberry Crush, and Blushing Pink. Her books have topped the Barnes & Noble Bestseller Lists and Book Sense's Top Ten, and her debut novel, Plum Girl, was a finalist for the Dorothy Parker Award of Excellence. Jill has also contributed essays to the anthologies *Flirting with Pride and Prejudice* and *Welcome to Wisteria Lane*. You can visit her online at: www.jillwinters.com.

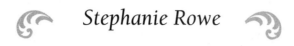

Stephanie Rowe

It's Not Luke's Stubble

PARIS: We're going to reveal the seedy underbelly of small towns—
starting with yours.
RORY: Stars Hollow does not have a "seedy underbelly." We don't
even have a meter maid. ("Richard in Stars Hollow," 2-12)

Stephanie Rowe grew up in New England and now lives on the West
Coast where she watches *Gilmore Girls*, not for Luke, she says, but because it's just like going home, right down to the ice on the puddles
and the ivy on the colleges.

'M BIASED.
Big time.
As in, hands-over-my-ears, I'm-not-listening-to-reason biased.
See, I grew up in New England. It's home. It's my roots.
Now, I live in the new and modern West Coast. Been there ten
years. I have to admit it's a pretty cool place to live, but it's not New
England. What is? Nothing. New England is special, unique, annoy-
ing as heck, and totally sigh-worthy.

And one of my favorite things about watching *Gilmore Girls* is that
it's chock-full of so many reminders of New England, and all the idiosyncrasies about the region that drive you so crazy at the same time
they ground you and let you know that you're H.O.M.E. We've got
intellectual elitism, Old Money, freezing ankles, history like you've
never seen before, traditions... the list is so long! Warms me up just
thinking about it....

Face it. The best thing about *Gilmore Girls* is not Luke's stubble.

Did You Steal That Class Ring?

One of the most beautifully annoying, aggravating, and wonderful things about New England is the intellectual snobbery. I mean, seriously, is there any place in the world that has a 1:5 ratio of people to colleges/universities? (I made up that stat, but I'm sure it's close.) Private high schools abound; Ivy League alumni reproduce like rabbits, permeating every sanctuary in the region; and everyone is judged based on where they went to school. And *Gilmore Girls* represents this intellectual elitism so well that I can barely keep from running upstairs and dusting off my diploma.

Take Chilton. Rory Gilmore headed off to her uniform-wearing private school when she was in high school and as smart as Rory was, she was no match for the total snobbery of that place. Oh, she was smarter than most of her classmates, but man, the sense of entitlement those kids at Chilton had was truly stirring. They owned the world, everyone else was a peon, and an Ivy League school was in all of their futures.

And prep school is just the beginning. What comes next? College, of course. Not just college. Top colleges. Top universities. New England is chock-full of all the best universities and colleges in the country. Except Stanford, and it doesn't count because…well…because it doesn't (it's not in New England, remember?).

When Rory was getting ready to do that college application tango, what schools were on her list? Yale and Harvard. That's it. Nothing else. And none of her classmates were dipping into the junior college or state school pool. Only the top of the top for Chilton kids.

And look at Richard Gilmore. Yale grad. Yale alum. Yale tattoo on his heart (well, how do you *know* he doesn't have one?). His granddaughter was considering Harvard? Crimson be damned! Only Yale was good enough for a Gilmore granddaughter. And as for the rest of the world? He and his warm and fuzzy wife Emily judge people based on whether they went to Yale. No other questions need be asked. Yale or no Yale, that is the question.

I lived that kind of educational snobbery. I breathed it. I basked in it.

Until I moved out to the West Coast, I didn't even realize any colleges other than New England schools existed. I mean, why would anyone go outside the region for school when we had the best there was to offer?

But now that I live out here on the West Coast (and I don't live in Beverly Hills, which might be different, so don't get up in my grill, okay?), I've discovered that smart people go to colleges I've never heard of. And they turn out okay. Go figure—what true-blue New Englander would have ever guessed? Very few people out here go to Ivy League schools, and that doesn't make them any less appealing as job candidates or dinner companions. Weirdest thing ever.... It's pretty cool, though, because I didn't go to an Ivy League school, and I always felt a little sub par because of it. Now I don't have to, which is good. But at the same time, I feel that something is missing out here. True education snobbery simply doesn't permeate society here the way it does in New England, and the flip side of that is how the importance of education just doesn't get the same kind of emphasis.

I may not have gone to an Ivy League school, but I know that it can open doors for you your whole life. The education, the contacts, the automatic stamp of credibility—it's all there for the graduates of those schools. For the folks who can't get in (like me), those schools still represent something to aspire to, to live up to—and, after college, to push to make up for. That kind of goal-setting is a fantastic thing, and it really helped me to continue to raise the bar for myself and accomplish more than I would have if I wasn't constantly reminded that I wasn't "the best."

And at the high school level out west...private schools are, well, not a big deal. They aren't elitist, they aren't for those of a "special class," not the way they are in New England. There's actually very few of them, and the ones that are there are, well, kind of normal. There's not that sense of everyone looking at your résumé to see where your diploma is from, not even in the job fields with the potential to really capitalize on the intellectual snobbery brigade (like lawyers, for example). I have friends who can afford private school for their children, and they don't even consider it. Didn't they get Richard's memo about the importance of private school? Apparently not. Does that make the kids out here take school less seriously? Some would argue not at all. I personally wonder if not having numerous high profile colleges, universities, and private schools around makes kids a little less driven to accomplish more and rise above where they are. I look back at my motivation level when I was a teenager, and, quite frankly, if I hadn't been surrounded by a bunch of prestigious education institutions, I'm not sure how motivated I would have been to work hard.

In New England, your alma mater isn't just key for jobs and memberships to golf clubs, it's also a resounding statement of your social worth as a person. On *Gilmore Girls*, where Emily and Richard have parties for Yale alumni, anyone who doesn't have that school on his or her résumé simply isn't worthy. Look at Jess, Rory's second boyfriend. Yeah, okay, so he was also kind of a jerk, but he wasn't worthy because he was just a common kid. But bring in Logan, her Yale boyfriend, and he's worthy? He treats Rory even worse than Jess did, in his own way, but that's okay because he's a Yalie. Even the show's producers give him more love than they gave Jess.

And Luke. Poor, gruff Luke. He gets no respect from Emily and Richard because he's got no résumé. He owns a diner, for heaven's sake. Where's the dignity in that? Yeah, that kind of judgment is wrong, but by having it happen to us or our friends, it helps teach us that it's wrong. It also helps force people to find their own worth, to laugh at the people who are unable to look beyond the surface. It makes us better people to have to deal with that kind of situation.

But for people like Luke, it's not just about the fact that he doesn't have the educational heritage; he also doesn't have Money.

Money, you say? He has money. He owns his own business.

Yes, but it's not Money. Big difference.

Money Makes the World Go 'Round

See, not only is intellectual snobbery thriving in New England, but in New England you've got people with Money, and they're something special. And Old Money is even better than New Money, because Old Money comes with a pedigree. New Money...well...you could still be too close to your unworthy roots. Old Money are class, they are history, they are It. More Money makes you Better. Old Money makes you Best.

Out here in the Pacific Northwest, there's not a lot of Old Money, because no one has lived here that long (at least not in comparison to New England). And there isn't even a lot of New Money, at least not the way there is in New England.

Look at Richard and Emily. Look at their ornate house, their proper manner of speaking, their refined and classy sense of dress, their sedate but expensive cars. Richard and Emily are Old Money, and they are better than anyone else. They are so far removed from the commoner that they can't even remember that their household staff are actually people. Real people don't have those kinds of jobs, do they? Ah, how lovely is that attitude? You just don't see that kind of snobbery in other parts of the country (well, there might be pockets, but it's still not *the same*, so I don't want any nasty reader letters, okay?).

I didn't grow up with Old Money, and there were many times that Old Money people liked to remind me of that fact by sneezing on me or pausing to use my pants to wipe the mud off their boots. There's nothing like a snub from an Old Money to humble you, and we all know humility is the key to happiness.

Look at the conflict between Richard and Emily and the life Lorelai has chosen to lead. Lorelai owns her own inn, has a diner-owner fiancé...er...ex-fiancé. She lives in an old house that always needs repairs and has less then ten bedrooms and *no* servants, and she drives a—gasp—*Jeep*. (Oh, and by the way, I had a Jeep when I was in college, and just so you know, there is *nothing* cooler than driving down the highway at ten o'clock at night in the pouring rain with the top off. People just think you *rock*. So, when it comes to the car thing, Emily and Richard are way off...Lorelai's so got the goods.) Richard and Emily believe their lives are worthy. Lorelai's is not.

But you and I know Lorelai is the one who's truly happy. She's the one with friends who love her no matter what. She's the one following her dream and accomplishing great things she can be proud of. But there's this firm belief on Richard and Emily's part that life is not complete unless you are in their Club (and that includes their country club as well). And quite frankly, you and I both know that Lorelai would never have found happiness and followed her dream if she hadn't been constantly trashed by Old Money and intellectual elitism. It made her stronger, pushed her to find her own beliefs, and helped her decide not to do to her child what was done to her. By growing up with "haves," she was able to make her own decisions about what was really worth having.

Richard and Emily are absolutely brilliant at keeping track of who is worthy and who isn't. Christopher—not exactly worthy, but better than pond scum. He has a bit of substance to his life résumé. Luke—so not worthy. Jess—so not worthy. Logan—worthy. Ironic, because Luke is the one who loves Lorelai and didn't leave her knocked up at age sixteen and then play MIA while his daughter was growing up (okay, he did do the MIA thing, but he didn't know he was a dad, so he's excused). And Logan, well, Logan's an underachieving, irresponsible, philandering snit—so not worthy of Rory, except, of course, for the fact that he's rich and "classy." But in New England, in the Old Money circles, love, devotion, common courtesy...those don't matter when evaluating a person's worth. Marry Logan for a few years. Marry Luke for a few years. See who makes you happier. You know true love and smiles in the morning will so get old. Servants, fancy cars, and black-tie cocktail parties? Enough to overcome anything.

Yeah...sure...like when Emily and Richard split, and Emily was living all alone in that big house. Remember when she came home from her date that night, shut the door, and started to cry? Her servants and her house totally made up for the fact that she was alone. Those were tears of joy to see her gorgeous antiques yet again...yeah ...that's it. Hey, let's be honest here. Emily's life is made complete by having Richard in it, and *Gilmore Girls* does a fantastic job of showing the snobbery and the elitism, and then pulling back the blinds and showing that life is really so much more than that.

Richard and Emily might seem to be a little over the top with their elitism, but they represent a class of people that's living and thriving in real world New England. You just can't find that kind of snobbery out west, not to that extent and certainly not as well-honed. Yes, there are times when it feels grating, but there's something reassuring about being in a world where education rules and your family tree matters. It's an idiosyncrasy other people might shun (and they'd have a good point), but to me, it's home.

All Those Related to Paul Revere, Please Raise Your Hand

Old Money being Best isn't just a reflection of money. Old Money is also about the immense amount of history and heritage in New England. Not just family crests, but history of the world, of America, of architecture.... New England is replete with a past and a history so phenomenally rich that it simply can't be duplicated anywhere else.

When I was in sixth grade, my history curriculum included a field trip every Thursday to a historic site. Do you realize how many field trips that is in a year? Yet there were no shortages of places to go. Paul Revere's house, the Old North Church (where the "one if by land, two if by sea" lantern would be hung), Sturbridge Village (a genuine colonial village with people working and "living" there), the State House, Plymouth Rock (where the Pilgrims landed)...it's truly amazing. The United States began in New England. The history is there for the taking, and it begins with the buildings.

Oh, the buildings. The houses in New England are old, classic, beautiful. Look at Lorelai's house. It's *cool*. It has character. A porch. A winding floor plan. Pipes that are so old they don't work unless Luke works his magic every so often. But the old houses aren't junk. They aren't broken down. They are well-kept, historical monuments. Oh, sure, your floor might be slanted and the windows might not open on hot days, and your heating bill might be astronomical because there are so many drafts in the place, but that's the kind of thing that warms the cockles of a New Englander's heart. These old New England houses have carvings on the door frames, they have amazing detail and designs on the lattice work on the outside, they have little round windows in turrets with carved railings on the roofs. They were built back in the day when people cared about making each building beautiful and unique. For heaven's sake, even Lorelai's *garage* has charm, with its cute little roof and its double doors.

And the churches in New England...wow. Do you know that when my mom and brother came to visit me out here, they commented that there weren't any churches because they thought they hadn't seen any? Well, there are, but they are usually squat and ugly, and some are even in schools and office buildings. No steeples, no stained glass, no history.

Just take a gander at the town of Stars Hollow, and you'll see that New England charm. The church, the town square, the gazebo, Lorelai's inn...these are buildings with a history, with a story to tell. With personality.

And how about Richard and Emily's house? Sure, it's a mansion, but it's not a *nouveau riche* kind of building or furnished with black metal couches and mirrored ceilings. Their fireplace, their fixtures, their furnishings...have you noticed the carvings on the walls? Or the trim? Their house is beautiful in the way that they used to make things before they decided that slapping up buildings as fast as they could was the way to go.

Walk down the street almost anywhere on the West Coast. Those houses are new. They have a certain look about them. A symmetry. A perfection. A total lack of character. Nothing like New England.

An old house in New England was built in 1650. An old house on the West Coast was built in the early 1900s, and even those are rare. It seems like most buildings were thrown up in the last thirty years, and it looks like it, too. Most of the old buildings out west *look* old. Run down. Outdated. The old buildings in New England look like treasured antiques that were designed and built with care and creativity, and their appeal has not only lasted over the years, but it has grown.

And the history of New England doesn't end with the buildings; it's in the meaning behind those buildings. The history of America is in New England, and that comes through so clearly on *Gilmore Girls*. Take the annual Revolutionary War reenactment in Stars Hollow, when the men dress up in costumes and replay the role that Stars Hollow had in the American Revolution (yeah, it wasn't much, but the reenactment is still powerful). Or when Taylor and Kirk wanted to rename all the streets in Stars Hollow by their original names. How cool is that? The street I live on out west is only fifteen years old and has had the same name the whole time. Um, yeah, high coolness factor there. And think about Emily's involvement in her Daughters of the American Revolution chapter. Again, we're talking a history that's way bigger than one little town. It's the history of our country, and it permeates New England.

And this history comes full circle back to our educational institutions. One reason New England schools are so deserving of their snobbery is their history. My high school was more than 100 years old. Yale? Founded in 1701. Harvard? Founded in 1638. Generations upon generations of the same family have attended these institutions. Look at Logan. His grandfather belonged to his Yale secret society (Life and Death Brigade, anyone?). So did his dad. And now, so does Logan. That's history, folks, and that deserves special treatment. Guess when Stanford was founded? 1891. Harvard has 253 more years of history than Stanford. The difference alone is more than twice Stanford's age.

Meet Me by the Gazebo at Midnight

It's not just the historical buildings that make the town of Stars Hollow a classic New England small town. Stars Hollow is a living, breathing entity unto itself, made of all the people who live there, its history, and its heritage. The people who live in Stars Hollow are connected to the town in their hearts and souls in a way that simply doesn't happen other places. The population of America is migrating west, so most of the people out here are originally from some place else. Half the people I work with out here are from New England! But in New England, most of the people have roots in the region. That gives them a rich sense of connection with the land and the community.

Even the physical layout of Stars Hollow is classic New England, with its delightful town square where all the celebrations and people-sightings occur. So many New England towns have places like these where the town comes together: a big grassy area, maybe a gazebo, trees that get decorated during the holiday season. You don't see that in new towns, designed to try to squeeze as many houses as possible onto a single plot of land. And without the town center, there's no central place to bring people together.

And the small-town characters...man...where do I start? Everyone in Stars Hollow is into everyone else's business, as well as the business of everyone who ever lived there. Like, when Luke and Lorelai started dating and the town became all upset because if they broke up, people would be forced to align their loyalties with one or the other of them, forcing half the town's population to stop eating at one of the two decent eateries in town. And the discussion descended into a recap of when the chocolate guy and the flower girl dated several decades ago and then broke up, forcing everyone to choose between chocolate and flowers for Valentine's Day. These kinds of intrusions into your personal life simply don't happen in the big cities, or in the transitional towns that have people moving in and moving out on a regular basis. You need a steady population base that cares about the other people in town to make this happen. In New England, you get that. On the West Coast, where people don't have the same kind of roots, you don't. Not to that extent.

Sigh.

Frostbite Is Sexy

And we can't forget about the weather. There is simply nothing like New England winters. Freezing cold. Gray and dingy. And, oh, the snow. How I miss the snow. Me and Lorelai, we're like twins. Remember the episode where the first snowflake of the season came down and she held up her face and basked in the glory of it? I so felt her love. There is nothing like that first snowflake of the season. The crisp, fresh air that seals your nostrils shut. That stillness of the air that is only present when snow is falling. It's magic. I don't care if you're four or forty or eighty-seven-and-a-half. That first snow, that first flake, is magic.

And it doesn't stop there. I completely understood Lorelai's pain when she stepped into that icy puddle and soaked her foot. I've done that! It's so awful, and miserable to be hustling into work with your foot slowly freezing off your body. And whenever someone rushes into Luke's diner, all huddled up because it's so cold that the sprint from the car to Luke's front door pretty much lays them out? Love it! There's nothing like that slam of frigid air when you step outside to wake a person up.

How fondly I recall sprinting from the restaurant to the car on a date in high school, huddled by the passenger-side door, my whole body shaking from the cold, *begging* my date to hurry and get the car open because I was *so* cold. Now *that's* bonding. Or the time I tried to stop my Jeep on a snowy road and slid right on down the hill until I came to a gentle stop in a snowdrift? I've used that story tons of times to bond with other people about driving in the snow. It's a *thing* that you get, or you don't. Out west you can't drive on the side of the road so your right tires compress the snow drifts. It just doesn't work the same way out here; I just end up giving myself a flat tire from side-swiping the cement curb.

On the temperate West Coast, schools get canceled at the *forecast* of snow (and I'm not exaggerating). No one owns heavy parkas or mittens (unless, of course, they ski, but that's another topic). No one even knows how to drive in the snow! Two inches of snow absolutely shuts down the city out here. Hello? Get some backbone!

You wouldn't see that happen in Stars Hollow. Throw on the snow tires, whip out the ice scraper to clean off your car, and have at it. And come on, where on the West Coast would Luke be able to make Lorelai her very own skating rink in her front yard? It was so sweet of him to give her the gift of skating to help her mend her relationship with snow after the tree fell on her car, a gesture of his true love for her. Out here, what kind of weather is there to bring a man and a woman together? Forty-degree rain? Seventy-degree sunshine? What's special about that? How does that kind of weather force a man to dig deep and face his feelings about his true love? It doesn't. Face it, if you want romance, you need the frigid icy cold of New England to make it happen. I'll bet the divorce rate is way lower in New England than anywhere else in the country. Misery bonds people. End of story. Well, I suppose earthquakes and volcanoes erupting would kind of rock the boat, but then you're talking about having to extract true love from a lot of dead bodies and rubble, and quite frankly, that's not all it's cracked up to be. Nope, give me a man who shovels out my Jeep for me and makes me a skating rink, and I'm a happy girl.

You Feel Incomplete, Don't You?

So, are you with me, or what? You're feeling the love for New England now, aren't you? You're wondering what school your neighbor graduated from, you're thinking that your daughter could use a little more appreciation for the power of prep school, you're envying the feeling of being so cold that your brain freezes, aren't you? And you're looking down the street at the ordinary houses, and your heart is aching for a town with history, right? You're even thinking the cold winters might not be so bad. See, home—the building or the place—isn't always about perfection. Home is about the imperfections that make it unique, that are familiar and cozy, that make you reach inside yourself and find strength and warmth you didn't know you had.

You might not be able to pack up and move to New England, but you can live vicariously by watching *Gilmore Girls*. Forget the witty dialogue. Forget the eye candy (mmm...Luke is sooo delicious).

Forget about wanting to gag T. J. because he's so annoying. Forget about wondering what job Kirk will have next. And definitely forget about wondering when Logan's going to grow up and be the man Rory deserves. Don't bother analyzing the three generations of mother/daughter relationships and figuring out how you can relate them to the women in your own life. Instead, bask in the all that is New England and feel the love.

Trust me. You'll never be the same.

Award-winning author **Stephanie Rowe** writes paranormal romance for Warner Books. She also writes teen fiction for girls under the name of Stephie Davis. For more information, visit Stephanie on the Web at www.stephanierowe.com or www.stephiedavis.com.

The Best Things in Life:
Food, Books, and Sex

Gregory Stevenson

Dining with the Gilmores

RORY: If the house was burning down, what would you save first,
the cake or me?
LORELAI: Not fair! The cake doesn't have legs! ("Red Light on the
Wedding Night," 2-3)

Somewhere in between talking and reading lies this show's third passion: Food. Luke cooks it, Taylor sells it, Emily and Richard barter tuition to get Lorelai and Rory to come eat it with them, and everybody
talks about it endlessly. In an effort to unpack the overload of grocer-
ies, Gregory Stevenson talks about what pudding, coffee, and Rice-a-
Roni mean to *Gilmore Girls*.

I AM A MOST UNLIKELY FAN of *Gilmore Girls*: a thirty-something, testosterone-fueled male whose ideal recreation involves
bruising football matches and obscure martial arts; a person who
any day would choose a horrible Steven Seagal movie over anything starring Meryl Streep. And yet I find myself enamored of this
family drama about mothers and daughters who do nothing but talk.
How do I explain this?

I attribute my fascination to two things: small-town community
and food. I grew up in a small town, so the close-knit identity and
wacky characters of the fictional Stars Hollow ring true to me. I come
from a town where nearly a thousand people, including the mayor,
attended the funeral of our local transvestite, who used to parade
around town in sneakers, a flowery dress, and a hat made from KFC
boxes. Suffice it to say that Kirk seems relatively normal to me.

Food is vitally important to small towns. Local eateries shape the
town's identity, while potlucks and shared meals provide a context for

social interaction. Residents show care to one another through the bringing of meals and desserts. Food is about more than sustenance: it is a means of communication.

Gilmore Girls establishes its interest in food from the very first episode, as the following conversation between Emily Gilmore and Lorelai Gilmore attests:

> EMILY: An education is the most important thing in the world, next to family.
> LORELAI: And pie. (Silence) Joke, joke. ("Pilot," 1-1)

But she's not joking. Food plays a role in Stars Hollow and in the lives of the Gilmores that rivals education and family. Stars Hollow is a town so in love with food that Al's Pancake World serves clams, the best egg foo young in town, and occasionally hosts a salute to Jamaica. Food almost serves as a character itself on *Gilmore Girls*. In particular, it functions as one of the show's primary means of communication. Food defines characters, becomes the vehicle for delivering the message of many episodes, and expresses the show's moral center and understanding of community. With each episode, *Gilmore Girls* offers up a smorgasbord of food for thought.

"Protestants Love Oatmeal"

When Sookie St. James learned of Rory Gilmore's acceptance at Chilton Academy, she said, "I'll make cookies. Protestants love oatmeal" ("Pilot," 1-1). Food defines people on *Gilmore Girls*. What they eat, how they eat, where they eat, and the way they cook reveals truth about their lives and their personalities. For Emily and Richard Gilmore, eating is a delicate art form and food a symbol of status and wealth. They never cook for themselves (that's what servants are for), and dinner must be eaten with decorum and etiquette. Their Friday night dinners with Lorelai and Rory offer up a menu (cassoulet, squab, escargot) that screams of sophistication and elitism.

By contrast, Lorelai and Rory's diet is a manifestation of Lorelai's desire to be as independent of her parents as possible. Like her mother, Lorelai almost never cooks, but for a completely different reason, finding even instant mashed potatoes to involve too much manual labor. As if in rebellion against high cuisine, Lorelai and Rory sustain themselves with their own version of the five basic food groups: pizza, cheeseburgers, Beefaroni, pie, and coffee. Fast food compliments their fast-paced lifestyle. Lorelai's reference to Tums as "amateur pills" ("A Deep-Fried Korean Thanksgiving," 3-9) reveals her pride in how her and Rory's healthy appetites symbolize their not only surviving, but thriving against the odds.

For Luke Danes, food identifies the duality of his character. This is a man who runs a greasy diner serving donuts, chili fries, and cheeseburgers, and yet is himself a health nut. Despite the unimpressive appearance of his diner, the food is outstanding. These contradictions symbolize the duality between what Luke projects on the outside—a gruff, belligerent, and uncharitable personality—and what he truly is on the inside—a sensitive softy who, despite his vocal protests, is always there when people need him.

Duality is also at play in the Kim household. The extreme health food approach of Mrs. Kim represents her ascetic outlook on life. For her, French fries are "the devil's starchy fingers" ("The Party's Over," 5-8) and the Cookie Monster a representation of one of the Seven Deadly Sins—gluttony. That she brought pamphlets on the evils of dancing along with her eggless egg salad to a charity dance reveals her position on the interconnection of physical and moral well-being ("They Shoot Gilmores, Don't They," 3-7). This forces Lane to exist in two worlds: her mother's Korean Christian world and her own American teenager world. That she has been known to wear a yellow "Trust God" T-shirt beneath a black "Dead Kennedy" T-shirt shows her attempt to walk this tightrope. Lane dutifully eats the tofu and kimchi her mother provides, but then sneaks off to Rory's for pizza and Snickers bars.

As chef and produce supplier, Sookie and Jackson employ food as their primary means of communication. They argue and bicker about food as though it is the only means through which they can reveal their true feelings. When Sookie first asked Jackson out on a date, their conversations about food suddenly became very awkward (meaning polite), because their relationship had become awkward ("Double Date," 1-12). Later, Sookie and Jackson experienced a rough patch in their marriage, and it was only when Lorelai witnessed them bickering over radishes that she concluded they had made up ("Last Week Fights, This Week Tights," 4-21).

In "Deep-Fried Korean Thanksgiving" (3-9), Lorelai and Rory got invited to four Thanksgiving dinners. Each one stood as a testimony to the character of its host(s): Mrs. Kim provided Tofurkey; Jackson deep-fried a turkey, to Sookie's endless disgust; Luke hosted his meal in the diner as though serving up bacon and eggs; and Emily and Richard had a ceremonial cutting of the turkey (one slice) before having it taken away into the kitchen for completion by the help. If the old maxim is true that "you are what you eat," then, on *Gilmore Girls*, identity is forged at the dinner table.

Sweetbread, Walnuts, and Dead Cows

Food is more than just salad dressing on *Gilmore Girls*. It plays an integral role in forwarding the plot and in communicating an episode's central ideas. When Sookie experienced pregnancy cravings, Jackson went out and bought her requested food, only to discover upon returning that she no longer desired it. Then Emily, separated from Richard, decided she wanted to date. She was craving a new life. Following her first date, though, she came home and cried. Like Sookie, she was craving something she didn't really want ("Emily Says Hello," 5-9). One Stars Hollow fundraiser called for bids on picnic baskets where the meal was to be shared between the bidder and the basket-maker. The hitch was that the bidder had to bid without seeing the contents. The baskets thus symbolized the uncertainty plaguing the relationships of Stars Hollow citizens. Jess outbid Dean for Rory's basket, and their subsequent meal underscored the uncertainty contained in any romantic triangle. Luke and Lorelai's meal hinted at the uncertainty of their relationship—was it friendship, or was it more? Sookie's basket represented her and Jackson's uncertainty about the status of their future. Only when Jackson went to great lengths to acquire Sookie's basket from the perennially basketless Kirk did he address the uncertainty and propose ("A-Tisket, A-Tasket," 2-13). Even rotten food plays a symbolic role. A foul odor in the town square got traced back to the fifty-nine rotting Easter eggs that had been missed during the previous week's hunt. Then, when Rory and a married Dean revealed their previously hidden affection for each other and Jason's dad revealed the secret news that Lorelai and Jason had been dating, we discovered the message of that episode: that some things shouldn't stay hidden, or they begin to smell ("Tick, Tick, Tick, Boom!" 4-18).

The use of food as a foreshadowing device is common on *Gilmore Girls*. Scenes involving food that occur near the beginnings of episodes often set up ideas or events that develop later. One such episode opened with Lorelai tasting cake samples for her and Max's wedding while Fran lectured her on the importance of choosing the right cake. By the end of the episode, Lorelai had broken off her engagement, determining that Max was just not the right piece of cake ("Red Light on the Wedding Night," 2-3).

Friday night dinners and Luke's diner serve as the primary locations for food consumption, so it comes as no surprise that the recipes offered up there often establish the recipe for the entire episode. An argument broke out at one Friday night dinner when Emily's cook put walnuts in the salad against her orders. When Emily decided to fire her, Lorelai related a meandering story with the following moral: "All I'm saying is sometimes eating a walnut is preferable to getting hacked to death or set on fire during dinner" ("Let the Games Begin," 3-8). The point was that sometimes fighting over the little things, like walnuts, just isn't worth it. That's good advice, and it was advice Luke, Lorelai, and Rory needed to learn. When Luke discovered Rory and Jess kissing in his apartment, he overreacted and tried to control their relationship—until he learned to let go of the little things. Then, when Richard deceived Rory into meeting with a Yale admissions advisor despite her longstanding preference for Harvard, Lorelai and Rory were furious. The episode ended, however, with Lorelai and Rory sitting in their respective bedrooms reading Yale brochures, having realized that sometimes it's better to just eat the walnuts ("Let the Games Begin").

At another Friday night dinner, Lorelai was enjoying an unidentified food—until it became identified. Emily informed her she was eating a dish with the decidedly pleasant name of "sweetbread," but which was in fact pancreas. This set up the central theme of the episode: that what appears pleasant on the outside might be something completely different underneath. This theme found expression in Paris Geller who, while doing an exposé on seemingly idyllic small towns, came to Stars Hollow with the goal of finding its seedy underbelly, as well as in Richard who, upon learning that Dean built a car for Rory, became convinced that, despite its shiny exterior, something was wrong under the hood. Richard's time in Stars Hollow also led him to the realization that his retirement, for all its hopeful promise, had turned out to be less than desirable. In these instances, Paris and Richard either sought or found the pancreas behind the sweetbread ("Richard in Stars Hollow," 2-12).

Luke's diner also establishes the recipe for episodes by setting up storylines or introducing themes. In the episode "One's Got Class and the Other One Dyes" (3-4), the theme of death received treatment in a figurative and playful way. The episode opened at Luke's diner with Lorelai telling Rory of her premonitions about her own death, which appropriately involved food (such as slipping on a banana peel and falling into a vat of whipped cream), and leading the viewer to expect Lorelai to experience some form of death. At that same moment, Luke brought them hamburgers which, for the first and only time in the series, he referred to as "dead cow." When Lane walked in, took a bite of Rory's dead cow, and then left, taking Rory's burger with her, it indicated that Lorelai and Lane would be linked in this episode by the theme of dying. Indeed, they proved to be the two individuals hinted at in the title of the episode, and what connected them was the episode's playful look at death. Thus, Lane, in an amusing wordplay on the concept of death (as represented in the title), went on to "dye" her hair purple in an act of defiance against her mother, while Lorelai, in fulfillment of her premonitions, figuratively "died" in her disastrous speech to a high school class.

In another instance, Lorelai complained about Luke changing the special on his blackboard to "Luke's Special Omelet." She ordered the omelet, but then frustrated Luke by proceeding to change everything special about it until it became an ordinary omelet. Thus, the theme was set: changing a working recipe leads to frustration. Consequently, Lane got upset when a high school aptitude test confirmed that she should work in sales, thus altering the recipe for her life. Michel got upset when Lorelai told his mother he didn't eat carbs, leading his mother to become more invasive in his life and changing the recipe for their relationship. Richard got upset when the school project he consulted on for Rory failed to win the contest, causing him to come to terms with how retirement had altered the recipe for his life. Finally, Dean got upset over how Rory's crush on Jess was changing the recipe for their romantic relationship ("Back in the Saddle Again," 2-18).

In "Emily In Wonderland" (1-19), Luke was bothered to see Lorelai and Rachel hanging out, as it represented an uncomfortable mixture of two women in his life. Later, when Rory asked Lorelai if she would ever be able to talk out her differences with her mother, Lorelai commented that she and Emily spoke different languages and simply didn't mix. Near the end of the episode, Rory and Lorelai ordered coffee at Luke's. After one sip, they both commented on how the coffee tasted different and then turned to look at Luke and Rachel, awareness dawning at how the addition of Rachel to the mixture was changing things. All this was set up near the beginning of the episode when Lorelai ordered pancakes and eggs at Luke's. Luke placed the eggs on top of the pancakes, inadvertently creating a breakfast face and freaking out Lorelai, who believed the eggs were ogling her. She insisted the two be separated because some things just don't mix.

The Chewy Moral Center

The moral vision of *Gilmore Girls* finds expression in the show's conception of community. The community of Stars Hollow bears the marks of reality: people bicker, hold grudges, invade each other's privacy, and occasionally lie to one another. Despite all this, Stars Hollow represents something of an ideal community. It is a place where citizens look out for each other, where church and synagogue share a building in peace and friendship, and where the entire town celebrates together and grieves together. After their break-up, Lorelai lamented that she had thought Max would be the "one person who would always be there for me." Yet after witnessing how the town rallied around her in her time of need, she realized that it was actually the townspeople who would always be there for her and, consequently, she for them ("Run Away, Little Boy," 2-9).

The morality of community that we see in *Gilmore Girls* is a secular morality, as the show is distinctively non-religious; yet this secular morality has a clear analogy in the apostle Paul's letter to the Philippians. Exploring this analogy may allow us to see the dynamics of community on *Gilmore Girls* in a clearer light. Paul wrote to a community characterized by disunity and internal conflict. In encouraging them to get along with one another, he distinguished between behavior that destroys community (selfish ambition) and that which builds it up (self-sacrifice). He counseled them: "Do nothing out of selfish ambition or vain conceit, but in humility consider others better than yourselves. Each of you should look not only to your own interests, but also to the interests of others" (Phil. 2: 3–4 NIV). Paul then argued that this model of exalting the interests of others over one's own finds its supreme example in Jesus Christ, who gave up equality with God (his own interest) in order to become human and die for others (Phil. 2: 5–8 NIV). In exhorting his readers to adopt the same attitude as Jesus, Paul provided them examples of others within their community who had done just that. This included Timothy who, in contrast to those who look out for themselves, actually "takes a genuine interest in your welfare" (Phil. 2: 20–21 NIV); or Epaphroditus who, while ill and practically on his deathbed, was more concerned about how his illness would affect the Philippian community than he was about his own condition (Phil. 2: 25–30 NIV).

This model laid out by Paul (selfish ambition versus selfless concern for others) is the same model that governs the secular conception of community in *Gilmore Girls*. Emily, Richard, and Paris represent the epitome of selfish ambition. Emily, a woman who holds a grudge like Kim Jong Il, does nothing without an ulterior motive. This is a woman who, upon being asked for a favor by her daughter, offered a list of demands in return, proclaiming, "Otherwise, I'm sorry, we can't help you" ("Pilot," 1-1). Status and societal position govern her and Richard's world. Selling out a trusted friend for a business advantage, petitioning the homeowner's association to stop neighbors from upstaging their full-size candy bars by giving out king-size ones at Halloween, or having a member of a church group bumped off a flight so Emily could make a last-minute pleasure trip to Europe is child's play to them. In fact, upon learning that Rory wanted to go as well, Emily gleefully called her travel agent to have her "bump another Baptist" ("Say Goodbye to Daisy Miller," 5-1). Likewise, Paris is a whirling tornado of self-involvement who never does a good deed unless it will look good on a Harvard application or job résumé.

These three characters try to worm their way into Lorelai and Rory's lives, but their own selfish actions and attitudes continually keep themselves at a distance. When they visit Stars Hollow, they stand out as outsiders, not because they don't live there, but because they don't fit in. Selfish ambition can exclude one from community. Taylor Doose is a good example. Although a lifetime citizen of Stars Hollow, his love of power and obsession with self-interest isolates him. When Jackson ran against him for town selectman, Taylor lost in a landslide and we saw him sitting alone in his store, in contrast to the huge crowd of people surrounding Jackson in the park ("Tippecanoe and Taylor, Too," 5-4).

In Paris's case, she gradually becomes more enmeshed in Rory's life, largely due to Rory's tolerance of her behavior. In fact, Rory's comparative selflessness has a positive effect on Paris. Occasionally, Paris will act on behalf of Rory's best interests (particularly when they do not conflict with her own), and doing so strengthens their friendship. Yet Paris's selfish ambition continues to keep her somewhat on the outside looking in on Rory's world.

If selfish ambition excludes, selfless concern for others defines community, as best represented by Lorelai, Rory, and Luke. In contrast to Emily's always-conditional actions, Lorelai and Rory share a relationship of unconditional love. They sacrifice everything for each other—social lives, time, even concert seats. At times they fight, but their ultimate concern is always the welfare of the other. What most distinguishes Lorelai and Rory from Emily is not their rejection of her elitist ways, but their willingness to look out for her interests even though she rarely reciprocates in kind. When Emily attempted to mold Rory into her image with portrait sittings or coming out parties, Rory went along with it, despite her personal desire not to, simply because it would make her grandmother happy. When Lorelai found out that the magazine cover story on her new inn was going to include disparaging comments she made about her mother, she urged the interviewer to pull the story, showing a willingness to sacrifice much-needed exposure in order to spare her mother's feelings ("To Live and Let Diorama," 5-18).

No one in Stars Hollow, however, better exemplifies selfless concern for those he cares about than Luke. Consider the evidence. Luke not only does odd jobs for Lorelai for free, but regularly fixes things on her house without being asked. He loaned her $30,000, no questions asked, to help out with the inn ("Scene in a Mall," 4-15), and loaned her his truck for two days, despite needing it himself ("The

Lorelais' First Day at Yale," 4-2). When angry at her, he still shoveled snow from her walk ("In the Clamor and the Clangor," 4-11); when displeased by her fishing date with another guy, he nevertheless offered to lend her his rod and tackle box ("Lorelai Out of Water," 3-12). He paid money to keep Jess out of trouble ("Say Goodnight, Gracie," 3-20), and hunted down the final twelve misplaced Easter eggs in order to help Kirk out of a jam ("Tick, Tick, Tick, Boom!" 4-18). Luke's true character came out when Jess, who according to Luke only takes care of himself and never thinks about others, told Luke to adopt the same attitude. While trying to decide if Jess was right, Luke decided to go fix Lorelai's broken window—unasked ("Nag Hammadi is Where They Found the Gnostic Gospels," 4-13).

Since food is a great communicator on *Gilmore Girls*, we would expect it to communicate the show's conception of morality in community. We are not disappointed. Juxtaposition of dining scenes represents different perceptions of community and social interaction. In "Scene in a Mall" (4-15), Lorelai dragged Emily to a mall food court for lunch. Emily (a "food court virgin") showed obvious discomfort at eating in such a low-class environment, an environment in which Lorelai thrived. At lunch, Emily expressed a desire to have the closeness that Lorelai and Rory shared, oblivious to the fact that it was her ambition and lust for status that was creating distance. Later, the episode cut between two dining scenes: Emily and Richard, sitting about ten feet apart, eating a fancy meal and barely speaking, and Lorelai and Rory, sitting less than two feet apart at Luke's diner, eating pie and communicating well.

Morality on *Gilmore Girls* is a recipe containing equal parts of sacrifice, community, and selfless concern for others. Members of the Stars Hollow community demonstrate their concern for each other through the giving of food. Lorelai and Rory, for instance, are rarely allowed to experience an illness, a relationship break-up, or even to do a good deed without copious amounts of food coming their way in sympathy or gratitude. It is also the way they express love for each other. For Lorelai's birthday, Rory ordered a cake with double frosting, spelled out "Happy Birthday" on the kitchen table with Malamars, and commissioned the local pizzeria to try to create the world's biggest pizza, which eventually required a crane for transport ("Happy Birthday, Baby," 3-18).

Luke presents an intriguing example of how food communicates concern for others in the context of community. Luke is a person with a hard tootsie-roll exterior that masks a soft, chewy center. Where Lorelai and Rory are concerned, that hard exterior quickly melts away. He is their primary source of food (his diner regularly substitutes for their kitchen), and he uses that food to show his love, whether it's special meals to celebrate a birthday, chocolate chip pancakes in times of pain, or agreeing to let Lorelai pull linked sausages out of him for a Halloween skit. During one Christmas episode, Emily uninvited Lorelai to her annual Christmas party, thus depriving Lorelai of her beloved apple tarts. Lorelai said that the Christmas party represented the only holiday where she enjoyed going to her parents' house, indicating that the apple tarts represented good memories as much as good food. Despondent, Lorelai went to Luke's where, instead, she found solace in another food. Luke offered her a burger, in a later season described by Lorelai as "the food that sustains me" ("Help Wanted," 2-20). It being Christmas, however, Lorelai wanted something festive. Recognizing her sadness, Luke returned with an improvised Santa burger (a depiction of Santa made from Wonder Bread, ketchup, and cream cheese). Lorelai was clearly touched by his culinary show of concern: "No one has ever made me something quite this disgusting. I thank you" ("Forgiveness and Stuff," 1-10).

Luke's relationship with the other members of Stars Hollow is more complex. With them, the hard candy exterior remains largely intact. Luke fights with them, intimidates them, and generally acts as the town grump. Yet when the need is truly there, the soft, chewy center shows through. The Luke who constantly mocked Stars Hollow's Revolutionary War re-enactors is the same Luke who later brought them free coffee as they stood freezing in the snow ("Love and War and Snow," 1-8). Likewise, when Taylor brought his group of Christmas carolers into Luke's and requested free hot chocolate for all in the spirit of the season, Luke pointedly and gruffly refused. Just then, however, Lorelai got a call that her father was in the hospital. Without a moment's hesitation, Luke, leaving to drive Lorelai to the hospital, announced the diner was closed, that all food previously served was on him, and that Taylor could get all the hot chocolate he wanted ("Forgiveness and Stuff," 1-10).

Luke's treatment of the townspeople mirrors theirs of him. When

Luke's uncle Louie died, none of the citizens agreed to come to the funeral because none of them liked Louie. He was mean and belligerent and, some noted, Luke was just like him. Yet, one fundamental difference distinguished Luke from Louie: when push came to shove, Luke genuinely put the interests of the townspeople above his own. So when Luke and Lorelai returned to the diner after the funeral, they were greeted with a diner full of food and throngs of people there to celebrate a wake. Luke was touched that they finally decided to remember his uncle until Lorelai pointed out that the town was there for him, not for Louie ("Dead Uncles and Vegetables," 2-17).

Food, and another juxtaposition of dining scenes, represents also the forging or dissolution of relationships. Emily and Richard threw a fancy, catered tailgate party at a Yale football game that led to division between Emily and Richard and between Emily and Lorelai. Then Lorelai went out on a first date with Jason in which they ended up scrounging for food at a supermarket. When Lorelai wanted short Pringles cans and there were none on the aisle, Jason went to great lengths to locate them in a back room. Emily and Richard's fancy party was marked by selfishness and so led to the weakening of community, while Lorelai and Jason's improvised supermarket meal brought them closer together because Jason was looking out for her interests ("Ted Koppel's Big Night Out," 4-9).

In many episodes, food plays a prominent role in the plot as a symbol of selflessness. Oddly, the Danish is a particularly frequent symbol. When Lorelai's grandmother died, the Danish symbolized Lorelai's willingness to put aside her own needs in order to help her mother. Lorelai offered to bring Danish and help with the funeral arrangements, but Emily refused. But then Emily, clearly overwhelmed, asked for help, and Lorelai replied, "Two cherry Danish coming up" ("The Reigning Lorelai," 4-16). In "Nick & Nora/Sid & Nancy" (2-5), the Danish symbolized forgiveness and reconciliation. After a fight between Luke and Lorelai, Lorelai was afraid to go into Luke's on "Danish Day," knowing he would not sell her one. In frustration, Rory expressed the true meaning of the Danish, "So you guys had a fight, big deal.... What better day to make up than Danish Day, the happiest of all days. The day when we all say, 'Hey, let's forgive and forget over a nice Danish and a cup of coffee.'" Rory's wise words rang true. When Luke later encountered Lorelai, he demonstrated his forgiveness not with the traditional words, but by telling her to make sure she came to the diner the next day to get her Danish—even though the next day was not Danish Day.

Although Emily's default mode is selfish ambition, occasionally she attempts to exalt the interests of Lorelai and Rory over her own. When she does, those efforts find symbolic expression through food. At one Friday dinner in honor of Rory, Emily abandoned her typical high-brow fare and served Rory's favorite foods, Beefaroni and Twinkies—of course, she had them made from scratch ("Sadie, Sadie," 2-1). After all, Emily's descent into the lower class goes only so far. Still, being Emily, these good intentions often go awry. When she fixed mashed bananas on toast for a laid-up Lorelai, under the assumption that Lorelai used to like it when she was younger, it turned out as horribly as it had when Lorelai was a little girl ("Rory's Dance," 1-9).

The prime example of Emily attempting a measure of selflessness through culinary symbolism is pudding. At Friday dinner, Emily served pudding for dessert to a stunned Lorelai. The shock stemmed from the fact that Emily not only hated pudding, but viewed it as hospital food. For Lorelai, the pudding symbolized Emily putting someone else's interests above her own for once. So when Lorelai later took Emily shopping for Rory's birthday and Emily kept selecting gifts that she liked as opposed to what Rory would like, Lorelai counseled her to "Think pudding." It worked, but the effect was short-lived. Emily later acted in a selfish manner with respect to Rory, and Rory chose not to tell Lorelai about it "because of the pudding," as her conversation with Lane attested.

> RORY: My grandmother served us pudding the other night and then she went shopping with my mom and they didn't fight. I don't know, I mean, they never get along, and now suddenly they're getting along, and I know that if I told Mom about the invites she'd wig out and call Grandma and that would be the end of the pudding.
>
> LANE: You know you can buy pudding.

Of course you can buy pudding, but you cannot buy what the pudding symbolizes—selfless concern for another. Later in that episode, a petulant Emily refused to attend Rory's birthday party in Stars Hollow, prompting Lorelai to state, "So I guess the whole pudding thing was just a fluke, huh?" ("Rory's Birthday Parties," 1-6). Maybe, but when Emily later showed up at the party after all, she showed that there was hope for her yet.

To paraphrase Lane, anyone can buy pudding or pizza or a Danish pastry. But on *Gilmore Girls*, for all its celebration of cuisine, high and low, it's not really about the food. It's about what that food represents—the celebration of life and the joy of living in a community of people who, deep down, genuinely care for one another.

> **Gregory Stevenson** is professor of religion and Greek at Rochester College. After writing on archaeology and the Book of Revelation, he decided to spend valuable research time listening to music and watching television. Since then he has written on U2, Christianity and Hollywood, and *Buffy the Vampire Slayer*. His book *Televised Morality: The Case of Buffy the Vampire Slayer* was nominated for the Mr. Pointy award by *Slayage*.

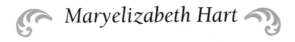

Maryelizabeth Hart

Reading, Rory, and Relationships

RORY: So you did read this before.
JESS: Yeah, about forty times.
RORY: I thought you said you didn't read much.
JESS: What is much? ("Nick & Nora/Sid & Nancy," 2-5)

Sullen, shaggy-haired Jess might have looked like the last thing he'd read was "pull tab to open," but the above bit of dialogue told viewers that he was going to fit in just fine with the Gilmore Girls. As Maryelizabeth Hart points out in her essay, this is a show where books and writing are shorthand for character and emotional development, and the one who reads and learns the most is Rory.

*"If you see a teen walking around with a halo
and a book, that's my daughter, Rory."*

—LORELAI GILMORE ("Eight O'Clock at the Oasis," 3-5)

THE WORLD OF *GILMORE GIRLS* is filled with bright, shiny, articulate characters who are thoroughly invested not only in popular culture via television, movies, and music, but also are tremendously well aware and informed of the written word, delivered in a variety of media. From the pilot's first scene at Luke's diner, with Lorelai's Kerouac reference passing right over the head of the clueless youth trying to pick up first her, then Rory, to the "Dorothy Parker Drank Here" production company logo at the end of every episode, the creative team has infused the Girls' world with literary significance.

In Stars Hollow, Hartford, New Haven, and elsewhere, we see readers reading—books, textbooks, magazines, and newspapers—on a regular basis. Characters visit the Black, White, and Read Bookstore (although mostly for movies), shop at the Stars Hollow Bookstore and library sales, and order books online. While books are clearly important to many of *Gilmore Girls's* main characters, it is Rory Gilmore, a.k.a. "The Thing That Reads A Lot" (1-4), who is at the heart of all of the show's literary references. Her relationship with words significantly helps shape and define her relationship with the rest of the world.

Volume I

As the show begins, Rory is deeply invested in her world of books— indeed, at this point in her relatively sheltered, small-town life, she lives in something of an ivory tower constructed of various tomes. Rory is not worldly; her small but intimate circle of friends is basically Lorelai and Lane. Rory's immersion shields her from real life. She doesn't even notice Dean's interest in her at first, because she is so lost in her reading. Early in their relationship, they exchange reading recommendations: Jane Austen for Hunter Thompson ("Love and War and Snow," 1-8). Rory's innocent assumption that Dean's love for her will extend to a love for the books she loves manifests itself in misplaced gifts (Lane points out that Kafka's *Metamorphosis* might not be everyone's dream romantic gift ["Forgiveness and Stuff,"1-10]) and pushing him to continue with Tolstoy when he suggests it might not be his cup of tea ("Star-Crossed Lovers and Other Strangers," 1-16). Like most youngsters in the blush of first love, Rory has faith in the generations of "true love conquers all" stories, but lacks the pragmatic interpersonal skills that might have helped her and Dean avoid some of their difficulties.

Rory recognizes that the best writers are also readers and has pragmatic reasons for indulging her passion. To fulfill her ambition to be the next Christiane Amanpour and work in international journalism, she needs a diverse background in more than punk bands and fifties movies—she needs a solid foundation of literary works to give her the best understanding of the historical and cultural context of her experiences. However, she is still shielding herself from fully experiencing the world, as evidenced by her reading in the school cafeteria and packing a book in her purse to attend a Chilton party ("The Breakup, Part 2," 1-17). At Chilton she encounters Paris Geller, who doesn't just have an ivory tower of books, she has an entire fortress; Paris is Rory without Lorelai's influence to draw her out of her books and into the wider world.

Books provide a handy shorthand when Rory's mostly MIA father, Christopher, is first introduced to viewers. Christopher's offer to buy Rory the *Compact Oxford English Dictionary* she covets is sincere; his lack of ability to follow through on his good intentions is Christopher in a nutshell.

Words also draw Rory and her grandfather together—when the Gilmores first start their regular Friday night dinners, Rory and Richard bond over disappearing into a newspaper and their love of rare first editions. This shared interest sees them through golf games and family crises, including Richard's unexpected hospitalization—Rory sits by his hospital bed, reading him the financial papers ("Forgiveness and Stuff," 1-10).

Lorelai's relationship with Rory's Chilton English teacher, Max, is driven in part by books as well—Max's, specifically. When she and Max are caught between their mutual attraction and their concerns about their relationship, Max is inspired to action by the great works of literature he has spent a lifetime teaching ("Emily In Wonderland," 1-19). When he asks Lorelai to marry him, she says yes, but her inability to read Max's beloved copy of *Swann's Way* by Proust—a move Rory describes as "ambitious" ("Paris is Burning," 1-11)—is an early indication that their relationship won't make it to the altar.

Volume II

Richard's gift to Rory of H. L. Menken's works collected in *Crestomathy* at the beginning of season two isn't just intended to please his granddaughter or inspire her—it's meant as a statement of Richard and Emily's intentions that Rory fulfill her journalistic potential, and they don't plan to let Dean or anyone else get in her way ("P. S. I Lo...," 1-20). Maybe if Emily and Richard were privy to Dean's patience while watching Rory browse real and virtual bookstores for hours on end, despite his lack of interest in such activities, they would be more appreciative of his support.

On Rory and Lorelai's spontaneous Harvard trip (after Lorelai decides not to marry Max), Rory is actually stopped in her tracks by the weight of the school's multiple libraries and the centuries of accumulated books they contain. However, being Rory, she has already made a significant dent in the 13 million volume catalog, as Lorelai points out ("Richard in Stars Hollow," 2-12). Inspiring libraries, uninspired boyfriend—the stage is set for Jess to enter her life....

Jess arrives in Stars Hollow with just the essentials: clothes, books, and cigarettes. He "borrows" Rory's copy of *Howl* and begins his unorthodox courtship by adding his own notes to the famous beat poem ("Nick & Nora/Sid & Nancy," 2-5). Their next several encounters are a combination of comparing literary notes (e.g., the merits of Ayn Rand and Ernest Hemingway ["A-Tisket, A-Tasket," 2-13]), and Jess not-so-subtly denigrating Dean for not being a reader.

Jess's pursuit of Rory isn't lost on Dean. After he finds Rory and Jess having dinner together with Paris, Paris saves Rory from Dean's wrath by claiming she is interested in Jess—and points out to Rory that Jess's literary taste and ability to debate the merits of Beat writing, Jane Austen, and poetry do make him attractive ("There's the Rub," 2-16).

Paris and Rory's on-again, off-again friendship starts out the school year off-again, with Paris welcoming Rory to the world of journalistic jealousy by sabotaging her at every opportunity when Rory joins the Chilton newspaper, *The Franklin*. It's a challenge Rory rises to with admirable diplomacy thanks to her journalistic ambitions, however, and the two end up reluctant friends again mid-way through the season. This is despite Rory's tendency to be an inadvertent thorn in Paris's side, as when she is forcibly socialized by the concerned Chilton headmaster rather than being allowed to pursue her preferred lunchtime activity of solitary reading, and finds herself briefly courted by the school's elite social group, the Puffs, to which Paris desperately wants to belong ("Like Mother, Like Daughter," 2-7).

The headmaster isn't the only person interested in Rory's reading habits; the stash of books in her room is a repeated point of curiosity. Jess uses the excuse of searching for a copy of Salinger's *Franny & Zoë* among Rory's books to explain his presence in Rory's room to Lorelai, Richard admires her system on his visit to Stars Hollow, and Christopher's new girlfriend, Sherry, demands to see all the books based on Christopher's description of Rory.

Christopher, despite Sherry, begins to look more and more like a romantic option: he demonstrates his newfound maturity and reliability not only by honoring his commitment to escort Rory to her debutante function, but also by delivering on his promise and gifting her with her own *Oxford English Dictionary*, complete with an entry for "jiggy" ("Presenting Lorelai Gilmore," 2-6). He also finds time to support Lorelai's graduation with a gift basket that includes a (joke) copy of the famous job guide, *What Color Is Your Parachute?* Unfortunately for Lorelai, it's the incredibly perky and unexpectedly pregnant Sherry who's the beneficiary of the new and improved Christopher at the season's end.

Volume III

Rory, whose world is so tied to words, has spent the summer between seasons two and three unable to bring herself to communicate with Jess via letter or telephone. While talking to Paris about whether or not date Jamie could be potential boyfriend material, Rory describes the perfect boyfriend as one who "likes what you like, reads the same books," which is a better description of Jess than Dean, a fact she is not yet ready to admit to herself or anyone else, especially Jess ("Those Lazy-Hazy-Crazy Days," 3-1). Her antagonistic attitude towards Jess doesn't keep her from sniping at bimbette Shane, whose vocabulary includes the word "bloaty," in a parallel to Jess's criticisms of Dean ("One Has Class and the Other One Dyes," 3-4). After several more verbal confrontations worthy of Kate and Petruccio, Jess and Rory end their relationships with Shane and Dean to be together.

When Dean returns books and CDs to Rory after their breakup, he admits that her persistence and the "crazy books she pushed on [him]" have spurred him to apply to a four-year college after all ("That'll Do, Pig," 3-10). Once Rory and Jess start dating officially, Rory has some adjusting to do; although she knows Dean and Jess are very different people, her vision of dating Jess was based on her first experience. However, Jess isn't Dean with book lore—he's still as rebellious and anti-social as ever, pleasant to practically no one other than Rory. Rory entices him into agreeing to dine at the Gilmore's by being a "book tease," bribing him with a copy of *The Holy Barbarians*. After their abjectly wretched dinner with Emily, it's not clear if she actually gives him the book as promised or not ("Swan Song," 3-14). It's a bad sign for the future of their relationship, which ends particularly anticlimactically when Jess, at the end of the year, leaves town without telling Rory.

School, at least, is going well for Rory; she returns to Chilton as school vice president for her senior year. School president Paris's first objective is to oust the ancient librarian and remake the library according to her standards—a priority that doesn't sit well with class president Francie and the other Puffs ("Haunted Leg," 3-2). When Francie successfully drives a wedge between the president and VP, Rory's return to reading alone in the cafeteria seems to bring her less satisfaction than it used to ("I Solemnly Swear," 3-11). It's a first step away from her literary seclusion.

Books, we begin to learn, do have their limitations. Lorelai and Rory are invited to Sherry's baby shower, where Lorelai responds to Sherry's query about what books she read when she was pregnant with Rory with "Judy Blume's *Deenie*," a staple of high school girls everywhere in the 1980s ("Take the Deviled Eggs...," 3-6). Sherry is looking to books to help her in the months ahead, but pregnancy and giving birth cannot be learned from books alone. The same proves true of fishing; despite Lorelai's efforts with the fishing volumes from the library, it's Luke's hands-on teaching that prepares her for her date with Alex ("Lorelai Out of Water," 3-12).

That doesn't mean books still don't have their uses. When Lorelai struggles with a gift for Richard's birthday, Rory rescues her by wrapping the volumes of the *Complete History of the Peloponnesian War* in a bow tie. If only Emily had done the same; she, with her gift of a very nice humidor, is once again one-upped by her mother-in-law, the original Lorelai, who arranges for her son to receive his father's humidor, once owned by writer Victor Hugo ("That'll Do, Pig," 3-10).

Lorelai and Rory also find a few books particularly useful in preparing for their backpacking trip to Europe—their *Rough Guide* travel guides. After Rory's high school graduation (where Rory's valedictorian speech is filled with admiration for "Jane Austen, Eudora Welty, Patti Smith," the women who were responsible for her upbringing, through their writing, as much as her final figure of admiration, her mother), they end the season in a last-minute negotiation over packing for Europe—Rory will leave a few books behind, in exchange for Lorelai losing some of her boots ("Those Are Strings, Pinocchio," 3-22).

Volume IV

Rory and Lorelai return from Europe just barely in time to transport Rory, her books, mattress, and other goods to New Haven. At Yale, Rory is studying Hemingway and Fitzgerald, and delighting in the atmosphere and the chance to discuss "good books, bad books, really thick magazines" ("The Fundamental Things Apply," 4-5). But this season the show begins to move away from reading and towards writing, though unfortunately, Rory's first college attempts at writing rather than reading don't go as well as she would have liked. She and Paris are undergoing the intern process for the *Yale Daily News*, and while Paris despises the process but is confident in her own abilities, Rory struggles until she finds her own critical voice— a critical voice that leads a ballerina to write "Die, Jerk" on Suite 5's message board in response to an unflattering review.

This isn't the only time the written word has unintended consequences for a Gilmore: the original Lorelai, after moving into the neighborhood (much to Emily's dismay), dies. Lorelai and Emily find a carbon copy of a letter to Richard among Lorelai the First's things that expresses her dismay at Richard's choice of brides, a final straw that leaves Emily on the sofa in her dressing gown, reading *The Crimson Petal and the White* (a novel about a social climbing young prostitute and the hypocrisy of the upper class, appropriately) and abandoning all the very specific funeral arrangements outlined in her mother-in-law's will to her daughter ("The Reigning Lorelai," 4-16).

Back in Stars Hollow, books still feature heavily in Lorelai's life. She's buried in design books and magazines as she, Sookie, and Michel work towards opening the Dragonfly Inn. The stress of the undertaking wears on Lorelai, although she is excited at having a grown-up excuse to buy a pony, leading Luke to call her "National Velvet." But Luke's literary allusions can't hold a candle to those of Richard's new business partner and Lorelai's new flame, Jason Stiles, whose guest room is filled with hundreds of books. Still, while Jason may have the smarts to keep up with his Gilmore Girl, he also has more quirks and eccentricities than all the denizens of Stars Hollow put together, and ends up being an alienating factor between Lorelai and Richard and Emily. Not even his books can make up for that.

In the aftermath of her breakup with Jason, and Luke's recent divorce by mail, Lorelai tells Luke, "I see Dr. Phil books in our future" ("Luke Can See Her Face," 4-20). While Luke scoffs that it's not likely unless Dr. Phil starts appearing in home repair stores, after a challenge from Jess to address his love life, he picks up the *You're Not Alone/You Deserve Love* book, workbook, and tape set from Andrew's bookstore. Not only does the book help *him* take action, first asking Lorelai to be his date to Liz and T. J.'s wedding, then kissing her on the porch of the Dragonfly, but it also helps Jess voice his appreciation for Luke and his love for Rory (if clumsily), after Luke passes it on to him.

Volume V

Emily, on the outs with Richard despite Lorelai's efforts at reuniting them, is off to Europe at the beginning of season five, and invites Rory to accompany her. Lorelai endorses the idea, hoping it will give Rory some perspective on her and Dean's newly ignited adulterous affair, but Rory perceives it as Lorelai shipping her off to Europe like a character in a Henry James novel ("Say Goodbye to Daisy Miller," 5-1). With the Atlantic between them, Rory puts her thoughts on paper for Dean's eyes only—too bad Lindsay finds the letter and ends the marriage. There are risks involved in putting things in writing, Rory learns—something Lorelai could stand to learn as well: despite having a daughter who is studying journalism, Lorelai is unguarded in her tales of Emily during an interview about the Inn, and creates another rift between her and her mother.

At least Lorelai has Luke. When Richard invites Luke golfing to get to know his daughter's new boyfriend, books act as a yardstick for acceptability: Luke excuses his lack of golf skills to Richard by claiming he prefers reading—but he can't come up with "science fiction guy" Philip K. Dick's full name and is sent home with assigned reading of the *Iliad* and *Odyssey*, books that, presumably, would make him a more worthy addition to the Gilmore family ("You Jump, I Jump, Jack," 5-7). Luke's life, like his chosen reading material, is a far cry from what the Gilmores would have wanted for their daughter.

Richard, meanwhile, is reading a little too much. The first indication that he is not truly happy living in the poolhouse apart from Emily is when he tells Rory he has recently completed the six volumes of *The Decline and Fall of the Roman Empire* in addition to reading P. G. Wodehouse and Proust, revealing that he is *very* lonely indeed ("We Got Us a Pippi Virgin," 5-5). Still, Emily, eating a lonely omelet with only *The Portable Dorothy Parker* for companionship, is unyielding, until a stray dog brings them back together.

Rory's quest to become a journalist continues as she returns to Yale and her new room in Branford College, which has a courtyard that was praised by no less than poet Robert Frost. Branford College is also where she meets and immediately dislikes Logan Huntzberger. She is dismayed to then find him on staff at the *Yale Daily News*, where things are back in full swing, with Rory on features and Paris on religion. Logan, as heir to the Huntzberger newspaper empire, is on whatever he feels like doing—which, largely, is nothing. Rory is determined to make her mark and stumbles on the secretive Life and Death Brigade—but she can't get access for the scoop without Logan's help. Logan gets her full access to an LDB extravaganza, where she really comes into her own as an investigative reporter for the first time.

It's also through Logan that Rory is able to obtain an intern position at the *Stamford Gazette* with Logan's father, Mitchum Huntzberger, that ends with a performance review in which Mitchum tells Rory she doesn't have what it takes to have a successful career in journalism. While Rory's relationship with Logan began in part because of her love of words and her desire to make her living with them, because of him Rory ends up questioning her journalistic ambitions and deciding not to return to Yale against her mother's wishes, instead moving her books and clothes into her grandparents' poolhouse, vacated since Richard and Emily's reunion.

Volume VI

The first significant sign to Richard that perhaps Rory is not going to end up back at Yale by living in the poolhouse? When he brings up great books at dinner, and she hasn't read anything more significant than the DAR menu ("We've Got Magic to Do," 6-5). Despite his and

Emily's best intentions and Lorelai's tough love approach, it takes a visit from Jess just after her twenty-first birthday to give Rory the perspective she needs to regain her purpose in life: Jess has published a short novel, *The Subsect*, and is working for the small press that published it, while Rory parties with Logan and mirrors her grandmother's life of social obligations. Rory hasn't just had a taste of Logan's world of hedonism and wasted talents; she is embracing it full-time. Jess's book, a reminder of her lost ambitions, is enough to trigger a break with Logan and her grandparents, and a return to Yale as well as a solid relationship with her mother.

Rory has rediscovered her confidence in herself and remembered who *she* had intended Rory Gilmore to be. She returns to her old study habits, but with a stronger sense of self and a real desire to use books and words as tools to reach people rather than an excuse to isolate herself from them. When Paris's tyranny over the newsroom as editor causes the *Daily News* staff to revolt and dismiss her, Rory is ready to rise to the occasion; she is voted in as the new editor after saving the paper from missing an issue, with Logan's help, an act that mends fences between them after a long separation.

Rory's journalism savvy reunites another couple as well: Lorelai and Christopher have a proud parenting moment when Rory shines on her Young Voices of Journalism panel, the beginning of a renewed contact that will prove significant when Luke, thrown by the sudden appearance of his previously unknown daughter April (whose fondness for reading causes more than one person to question her paternity), fails to rise to Lorelai's marriage ultimatum at season's end.

Throughout the seasons, we see characters' personalities expressed and reflected in their relationships with the written word. Richard and Emily enjoy news periodicals and great works of literature suited to their station in life, but would not think to venture beyond those prescribed boundaries. Dean and Luke both think of books primarily as resources for information, and only secondarily as a form of entertainment, but they only ever flirt with reading, never engaging in a passionate relationship with it. Jess, in contrast, is defined by his relationship with books, first others' works, then the creation of his own and his support of others' through the publishing company. Paris is passionate about words in a different way, collecting knowledge like a finite resource and using her knowledge as a weapon to intimidate or impress others.

Lorelai's reading is enthusiastic and quirky, with occasional moments of dedicated concentration, reflecting her approach to life in general. She is equally capable of appreciating the works of Shakespeare, the poetry of Sylvia Plath, and an in-depth interview with a rock musician, and of picking and choosing the shiniest bits to add to her cultural repertoire. Lorelai delights in exercising her mind in less-than-conventional ways and in meeting the challenge of keeping up with her best friend, her very bright and erudite daughter, Rory—whose relationship with the written word tells us not only about her, but about the ways she has grown since season one.

Between her sophomore year of high school and her junior year of college, Rory has transitioned from a young woman with a passion and admiration for other writers' works to a young woman with the life experience and self-confidence to create and advocate her own. Sixteen-year-old Rory was invested in writing to meet others' expectations; twenty-one-year-old Rory is capable of accepting constructive criticism, but also respects the value of her own opinions, and of providing guidance to others in her role as editor. This Gilmore Girl has grown into a Gilmore Woman, who may not yet have all of life's answers but who will look to her beloved books as just one resource among many, including truths told through visual media, music, and her own adventures in the greater world, no longer shielded by the covers of a book.

Maryelizabeth Hart is co-owner of Mysterious Galaxy, an independent genre bookstore in San Diego, California. She co-authored companion books to *Buffy the Vampire Slayer* and *Angel* with husband Jeff Mariotte and regular Smart Pop contributor Nancy Holder. Her regular writing jobs are editor of the store's newsletter, and reviews contributor. She has been reading her whole life and remains passionate about books.

Kristen Kidder

"That's What You Get, Folks, For Makin' Whoopee"

RORY: They never invited their priest over to try and talk you out of having sex?

LORELAI: Five times! And on the last one, they triple-teamed with a priest, a rabbi, and a Mormon missionary. I made so many jokes that night I should have had a microphone and a brick wall behind me. ("He's Slippin' 'Em Bread...Dig?" 6-10)

You'd think a show based on an unwed mother and her teen-aged daughter would be a little loose around the moral edges, but the Gilmore Girls can't catch a break in their sex lives. It's not just that nobody in the show can maintain a relationship; as Kristen Kidder points out, when Paris, Rory, and Lane finally move on to makin' it, the show makes them pay for it, too.

HAVING A BABY CHANGES *EVERYTHING*. At least it does according to Johnson & Johnson, whose advertisements—fuzzy, thirty-second Valentines to parenthood—punctuated the commercial breaks throughout *Gilmore Girls's* seven seasons. According to the company's Web site, the concept behind these public service announcements (and really, what else would you call them? No specific product was ever mentioned) is simple: "You were once the center of your universe and now your baby is. Johnson & Johnson understands." An interesting campaign choice for a television show marketed to teenagers.

Which is not to say that *Girls* is just, well, for girls. As I enter the third decade of my life I have to admit, Tony the Tiger witness-protection-program style, that I rarely miss an episode of the show. But while I may not be an anomaly, flashy Web sites, contrived marketing tie-ins, and (lately) that infuriating teenage gab fest during commercial breaks confirm that I and my rapidly maturing ovaries are no longer members of the CW's target audience. Which calls the intentions of the network's pro-parenting propaganda into question, especially when you consider that *Gilmore Girls* was originally developed through the advertiser-funded Family Friendly Programming Forum's (FFPF) Script Development Initiative, a group that encourages the television community to produce more primetime shows that families can enjoy watching together. Synergistic shocker: Johnson & Johnson, the company synonymous with responsible parenting, is a member of the coalition.

All of which makes for a tricky, if largely innocuous, mixed message towards sex and childrearing. The "Changes Everything" ad campaign is at once minimalist and perplexing; in fact, the video is little more than black-and-white home movies of chubby, laughing babies with a voiceover that poses inane rhetorical questions like, "Remember the days when you spent hours trying to look glamorous? So who'd have ever thought someday you'd rather spend hours trying to look silly?" and, "There was a time when poker night was what you looked forward to all week. So who'd have ever thought boys night out wouldn't hold a candle to boys night in?" Call them what you want—adorable, trite, and propagandist are all adjectives that may come to mind—but these advertisements are undeniably effective. And ostensibly directed towards older adults.

So why would these images pepper *Gilmore Girls*, the CW's love song to unconventional parenting? From the outset, Lorelai Gilmore flouts all stereotypes of the teenage mother. Having a baby no doubt "changed everything" for her, but Rory's birth is positioned within the show's narrative as the catalyst for positive change. As an adult, Lorelai's relationship with Richard and Emily is tenuous at best; flashbacks to her childhood depict a deeply dysfunctional family with radically different values. The pregnancy not only saved Lorelai from the stifling life of a well-to-do New Englander (stomachs bloated with child do not go well with cotillion dresses), but it also gave her a chance to escape from what she perceived to be a never-ending cycle of snobbery and privilege.

To be fair, *Gilmore Girls* does not let Lorelai off the hook completely for breaking away from her family's millions. There are those lean years that are alluded to every now and then—the ones she spent as a chambermaid at the Independence Inn, estranged from her parents and living with her young daughter in a tool-shed-turned-guesthouse in the back. But Lorelai Gilmore is nothing if not plucky and determined: she worked her way up to manager, raised a straight-A student, fell in and out of love, and earned her business degree at night. When the Independence Inn burned down in season three, she seized the opportunity to open the Dragonfly, a bed and breakfast she runs with her best friend. Again and again, *Gilmore Girls* assures us that Rory's birth did not signal the end of her mother's opportunities for success—which is likely one reason why the show consistently receives top billing from the National Organization for Women's Feminist Primetime Report—but that conclusion is very much at odds with established cultural wisdom, which is likely to make the folks over at FFPF a little nervous.

Case in point: Johnson & Johnson's ads insinuate that babies are the end of frivolity, of nights out with the boys. It stands to reason, therefore, that they are aimed at people who still hold these pastimes dear—namely teenagers and young twenty-somethings. In this way, the campaign functions as a sort of system of checks and balances—we are reminded, as we make our way to the refrigerator during commercial breaks, that perhaps there is more to life as a single mother than razor-sharp comebacks and coffee breaks. To be sure, the babies in the Johnson & Johnson ads appear innocuous, but the company's equation of children with sacrifice—both personal and financial—is legitimate (and something that is routinely glossed over in *Girls* or rendered irrelevant by the untold personal fortunes of Rory's grandparents and, in later seasons, her father).

Unrealistic portrayals of sex and parenting are not uncommon in teenage soap operas like *The O.C.* or *Dawson's Creek*, but they take us by surprise in *Gilmore Girls*—namely because the population of Stars Hollow seems to consist almost entirely of intelligent, interesting, and complicated female characters. While many of the show's running gags are based firmly in hyperbole (been to a town meeting lately?), one would assume that *Gilmore Girls*'s feminist-friendly street cred would render it immune to many of the pitfalls of mainstream serial dramas. (Let's just say I'm willing to make a fairly significant wager that if one of the main characters ever got pregnant, it's doubtful that the situation would be "taken care of" by a fall down the stairs or an impeccably timed miscarriage.) *Girls* must be doing something right to earn the highly coveted NOW seal of approval.

Yet, we find again and again that these accolades do not automatically translate into "mother knows best"; throughout the series Rory is positioned as the more responsible, level-headed Gilmore. She's the one who packs the map on road trips, who once self-identified as "not spring-breaky" ("Girls in Bikinis, Boys Doin' the Twist," 4-17) and who recently cautioned her mother as she embarked on a somewhat ill-advised rebound romance with her baby's daddy: "I don't want to see you get hurt again. I just want you to be careful" (to which Lorelai quips, "Is this the safe sex talk again?") ("'S Wonderful, 'S Marvelous," 7-4). In fact, Lorelai's relatively care- and consequence-free attitudes towards sex have largely escaped the younger generation of women on the show, all of whom have had relatively traumatic first sexual experiences. If the CW was afraid that *Gilmore Girls* made young love look too much like fun and games, they needn't have worried: watching just one of the defloration episodes is enough to make you want to cross your legs and wait out puberty—preferably in a nunnery.

Gilmore Girls's first foray into teenage sex occurred mid-way through season three, as Rory and Paris waited for college acceptance letters and competed for the honor of giving a speech at Chilton's bicentennial, to be televised on C-SPAN. The episode—aptly titled "The Big One" (3-16)—was teased on every conceivable media outlet for a week: in a bedroom heart-to-heart Rory was shown confessing to her prep-school friend that "it's just time," leading viewers to believe that she had finally given it up to Jess, Stars Hollow's answer to James Dean. But come Tuesday, *Girls* fans were shocked to discover that her actual line was "It's just *not* the time," confirming the teenager's virginity to her friend, her loyal viewers, and, as it turns out, her eavesdropping mother. But the network's build-up wasn't all for naught: the episode did recount a first sexual experience—except we found out that it was Paris, not Rory, who did the deed.

This kind of bait-and-switch tactic is not unusual in television promos (especially during sweeps week). Neither is the fact that the main character was spared the burden of sexuality. What's shocking is that the implied consequence of this decision (and in teen drama, sex always has a consequence) is not pregnancy, an STD, or social alienation—it's rejection from the Ivy League. In a subsequent scene we watched as Paris began to melt down at the podium in the middle of her bicentennial speech. She ranted, in part: "I'm being punished. I had sex, so now I don't get to go to Harvard. [Rory's] never had sex. She'll probably go to Harvard; she's a shoo-in" ("The Big One," 3-16). To be fair, Paris has a tendency to display judgments that are a little, well, insane. (Not coincidentally, her background and attitudes mirror those of Richard and Emily—confirming yet again that Lorelai's break from that lifestyle was a positive change.) Still, it was jarring dialogue from a television show that is almost universally lauded by feminists and respected women's organizations—especially one that is addressing teenage sex directly for the first time.

Except: it's possible to dismiss Paris's tirade as the devastation-born ravings of a scorned overachiever. After all, *Girls* creator Amy Sherman-Palladino, who wrote this episode, is known for her endearing propensity towards neurotic characterizations; perhaps we can chalk the whole episode up to satire (a theory that is supported by the repeated assurances from Rory—ever the voice of rationality—that this rejection was not a reflection of Paris's morals). Yet the virginal Rory came home that night to find acceptance letters from Harvard, Yale, and Princeton in her mailbox. And Lorelai still sang to herself, "I've got the good kid," when she learned that it was Paris, not Rory, who had made the decision to become sexually active ("The Big One").

Talk about a mixed message.

Luckily for Paris, the loss of one's virginity does not preclude a girl from admission to *every* Ivy League school on the East Coast, and by season four both she and Rory were firmly ensconced at Yale. Co-ed clichés abound, and before you can say "finals week" Paris was in a relationship with a *much* older professor and Rory was forced to acknowledge that she was in the middle of a serious dating slump—you know there's a problem when you're photographed with the lunch ladies for your roommate's end-of-the-year collage. This realization hit hard, causing Rory to spend the first day of summer vacation waxing nostalgic to Lane about the one who got away. In this scenario "the one" was, of course, the newly married Dean—when faced with a serious emotional crisis what teenage girl doesn't long for the security of her most dependable ex?

All of which soon became window dressing for a climactic re-telling of the world's oldest story. Life as a newlywed was apparently not working out well for Dean. His wife didn't understand him. He couldn't seem to make her happy. Every waking hour was miserable. With only the weakest of monosyllabic protests, Rory applied herself to the situation like a poultice and the high school sweethearts reconnected—in the most biblical sense—in the season finale, amid the mournful chords of Lou Reed's "Satellite of Love." (Say what you want about those Gilmore Girls—they always have the appropriate soundtrack for life's biggest moments.)

And yet, Rory was surprisingly naïve for an adulterer. When the unannounced return of her mother put a hasty end to the lovers' idyll—sweaters were rumpled and excuses were offered and for a minute the whole scene was reminiscent of a seedy romantic comedy—Rory had the temerity to believe that people would be happy for her, even embrace her decision. While she apologized first for not consulting her mother before making this giant leap into adulthood, Rory concluded her justification speech with the world's best rhetorical question: "Aren't you glad it happened with someone who's good and who really loves me?" ("Raincoats and Recipes," 4-22). The idea is so preposterous you could almost feel the audience stammer in unison in response with Lorelai: "Um, remember Lindsay? His *wife*?!?"

Still, apart from the whole Dean-being-married thing, Rory's first sexual experience was in many ways worthy of emulation: she waited until she was in her late teens, her partner was a long-term boyfriend, the couple practiced safer sex, and she maintained open communication about her decision with an adult she trusts. Still, too, Lorelai's explosive reaction to her daughter's decision was understandable, although unprecedented in the context of their relationship: "I didn't raise you to be like this," she responded furiously. "I didn't raise you to be the kind of girl who sleeps with someone else's husband" ("Raincoats and Recipes"). For Rory, the disapproval of her mother is worse than rejection from the Ivy League, and the episode concluded with her crumpled on the front lawn, sobbing and alone, the morning-after glow a distant memory.

Significantly, Lorelai made no effort to comfort Rory in the minutes immediately following their confrontation; in fact, the image of her holding back from her increasingly hysterical daughter concluded season four. While this is not an uncommon parenting technique—after all, the kid has to have some time to reflect on what she's done—the loss of Rory's virginity punctured the veneer of the Gilmore Girls' otherwise pristine relationship. Fighting and bickering became more common in the following years, epitomized by a temporary (although traumatizing) estrangement in season six. While it's significant that these changes in their relationship coincided with the advent of a little nookie (Lorelai also wasn't thrilled when Rory starting sleeping with Logan before he was officially boyfriended), they could also be credited to the normal mother/daughter shifts typical of adolescence—perhaps the Gilmores just hit their rough patch later than most.

Last up on the virginity trifecta is Lane, Rory's long-suffering best friend. Lane has perhaps had the most trying romantic history of all the women on *Gilmore Girls;* throughout high school, her Seventh Day Adventist mother restricted her access to everything from music to junk food to boys. Although Lane rebelled whenever and wherever she could, as it turned out her mother did convince her of one thing: that she should wait until she's safely under the auspice of marriage to have sex, an ideology that spewed out of her like a robotic bolt of lightening when her boyfriend and bandmate Zack made his first overt play for her pants. His moves, adorably enough, consisted of spaghetti dinner with Ragu and Pepsi, eaten on the living room floor. Ever a trooper, Lane started in on the dishes immediately after shooting him down: "You're not getting any tonight," she deadpanned. "The least I could do is clean up" ("So...Good Talk," 5-16).

Lane found her own embrace of abstinence more than a little troubling ("Why couldn't the gluten-free thing stick?" she sighed to Rory. "I could have lived with that" ["So...Good Talk"]), but still, she waited, even as her contemporaries fell in and out of love—and jumped in and out beds. But in season six, just when she seemed to have gotten the hang of playing the Donna Martin to Rory's Kelly Taylor, Lane and Zack got hitched. So while it might not be very punk rock to be too young to drink legally at your own wedding, it's certainly handy to have the thumbs up from God to get laid.

Except we found that even newly married young women—including those who can legitimately wear a virginal white gown as they walk down the aisle—are not immune to the *Girls*'s first-time curse. Lane returned from her honeymoon in Mexico with both the stomach flu and a shocking conviction that "sex sucks so bad. Sex sucks worse than I thought" ("That's What You Get, Folks, For Makin' Whoopee," 7-2). Granted, the one and only time she and her new husband did the deed they were attempting to recreate that scene in *From Here to Eternity* (bonus points to the tweener viewers who caught that cinematic reference), a feat that could make even the most experienced among us a little uncomfortable. Still, Lane's newly formed convictions regarding the evils of the flesh rivaled her repressed mother's: barely in her twenties and she's at peace with the fact that hers will likely be a sexless marriage. (In fact, Mrs. Kim maintained that she only had sex once, confirming—without irony—that she got "lucky" the first time.) Nothing, it seemed—not even assurances from Rory that sex is great and that she and Zack should try it again—would change Lane's mind.

And still it gets worse. A quick trip to the doctor confirmed that the "parasite" she brought back from Mexico was not Montezuma's Revenge but the early stages of pregnancy, knowledge that Lane quickly crystallizes into the following maxim: "I guess the combination of salt water and seaweed and discount Mexican condoms and terrible, terrible sex leads to a baby." To which Rory replied, in a tone worthy of the best after-school special, "You only did it one time, and wow, a baby" ("That's What You Get, Folks, For Makin' Whoopee"). Is there a more effective way to keep teenagers' legs closed? I didn't think so.

So here we are, season seven. And yeah, Johnson & Johnson, we get it: having a baby changes *everything*. Few could argue that the reality of single motherhood is as effortless as Lorelai Gilmore makes it appear; many viewers don't have the resources at their disposable to make ends meet, never mind send their children to private schools and open new businesses. A healthy dose of counter perspective is not only fair, it is—including looking at a couple of those other potential consequences—warranted. But there's a fine line between telling it like it is and scaring young women away from sex.

It is somewhat ironic that on *Gilmore Girls*—a show whose very existence can be credited to the effects of adolescent hormones on overdrive—the shedding of virginity is equated with loss, and not just of one's hymen and an at-times cumbersome social label. The consequences of sex for Paris, Rory, and Lane were no doubt presented as comical hyperbole, but they were dire—and robbed each young woman of the thing she cherished the most. The overachieving Paris was denied entry to her first choice college, the first fissures in Rory's relationship with her mother were formed, and Lane's carefree rock 'n' roll days were abruptly ended. Of course, these simplistic cause-and-effect scenarios have little to do with real-life sexuality, but that matters little in the world of teenage dramedy. And while it's unclear how much of this ideology can be credited to the influence of the Family Friendly Programming Forum, it's important to remember that Family Friendly doesn't automatically equal Female Friendly. Not even *Gilmore Girls* is immune to the pressures of a conservative think tank.

That's what you get, folks, for makin' whoopee. I guess no one understands that better than the women of Stars Hollow.

Kristen Kidder is a writer, cultural scholar, and recovering academic who lives in Brooklyn, New York. In the last seven years, she has only missed one episode of the *Gilmore Girls*.

There's Reality and Then There's Lorelai: Gilmore Girls and the Real World

Chris McCubbin

Golden Age Gilmore Girls
How Classic Hollywood Comedy
Defines the Show

LORELAI: So I've decided I'm saving myself for William Holden.
RORY: Wow, it's nice out here in left field.
LORELAI: Hey, I'm sorry. *Sunset Boulevard* was on last night, and I
don't know...I've known him for years—*Sabrina, Stalag 17*—
and yet last night something snapped. ("A-Tisket, A-Tasket," 2-
13)

Gilmore Girls has roots firmly planted in the fast-talking screwball
comedies of the 1930s and '40s, and in this essay Chris McCubbin analyzes in detail just how deep those roots go...and what a great Lorelai Katharine Hepburn would have been.

Gilmore Girls, 1952 D. HOWARD HAWKS

STARRING: **Katharine Hepburn** (LORELAI), **Audrey Hepburn** (RORY), **William
Holden** (LUKE), **Cliff Robertson** (CHRISTOPHER)

WITH: **Agnes Moorehead** (EMILY), **Edmond Gwenn** (RICHARD), **Tab Hunter**
(DEAN), **Harold Peary** (TAYLOR), **Shirley Booth** (BABETTE), **Kathleen Free-
man** (MISS PATTY), **Alvy More** (KIRK), **Vivian Vance** (SOOKIE), **Mary Grace
Canfield** (PARIS).

This modest but likeable comedy is notable for being the only screen
pairing of Katharine and Audrey Hepburn. Playing mother and daughter,
the two actresses display a surprising chemistry, assisted by a sparkling
script that evokes the verbal acrobatics of *Bringing Up Baby*.

Lorelai Gilmore (K. Hepburn) is a girl from a rich family who eloped as a teenager against her parents' wishes. Widowed at a young age with a baby daughter, she refused her parents' help and took a job at an inn to support herself. As the movie opens, young Rory (A. Hepburn) is sixteen, and Lorelai, against her better judgment, reconnects with her aristocratic parents (Gwenn, Moorehead) to secure their help with the girl's education. Romantic complications arise when Lorelai's parents try to match her up with Christopher (Robertson), the charming but dissolute younger brother of her deceased husband, forcing Lorelai to face her attraction to the poor-but-honest Luke (Holden). Meanwhile, Rory is discovering her own first love with local boy Dean (Hunter).

The film is enlivened by a fine selection of character actors playing the Gilmores' quirky neighbors in the bucolic village of Stars Hollow. Holden displays his comedic gifts in a subplot about his ongoing rivalry with overblown town selectman Taylor (Peary).

No, the movie described above never existed (and, in fact, couldn't possibly have existed—a few ages and career dates are fudged, and the '50s studio system would have certainly made it impossible for all the actors listed above to have worked together on the same movie). But it seems to me that the first six seasons of *Gilmore Girls* are Amy Sherman-Palladino's attempt to make this fantasy movie a reality. From top to bottom, *Gilmore Girls* is suffused with a style and sensibility drawn straight from Hollywood comedies of the 1930s, '40s, and '50s.

There are, of course, some significant differences between our imaginary romantic comedy and the TV series. Lorelai becomes a widow, and Christopher becomes Rory's uncle, because the Hays Production Code (adopted in 1930 and in effect until 1967) would never have allowed an unwed mother to be the heroine of a movie ("The sanctity of the institution of marriage and the home shall be upheld. Pictures shall not infer that low forms of sex relationships are the accepted or common thing"—Hayes Production Code), and even a divorced mother would have been a bit dodgy.

Our movie also has no Lane Kim. With the exception of Charlie Chan (not a beloved character among Asian-Americans), there were pretty much no assimilated Asian-Americans in films during the first half of the twentieth century. In the early '50s, with institutional racism high and American sensibilities regarding Asians still prickly from WWII and Korea, the idea of a perky, smart, and talented Korean-American teenager would have been simply unthinkable. Instead, Rory's best friend might have been a swing-loving daughter of a family who fled from, say, France or Spain to escape the spread of fascism. Likewise, there's no Michel; a character in a '50s movie could be French, or he could (rarely) be black, but he couldn't be both.

Some may argue with my choice of the Hepburns (Katharine and Audrey were effectively unrelated, despite a common aristocratic ancestor from the sixteenth century) as the spiritual avatars of Lorelai and Rory (and please do argue...that's the fun of imaginary casting games like this).

It's easy to defend Alexis Bledel's Rory as an evocation of Audrey Hepburn in, say, *Sabrina*; although Bledel is a bit more coltish and charmingly awkward than the eternally serene Hepburn, the two share a very similar self-possession and ethereal beauty.

Physically, Lauren Graham doesn't match up nearly as well with Katharine Hepburn. Graham has a softer and distinctly more feminine presence than the—let's face it—rather butch Hepburn, and doesn't really approach Hepburn's crackling intensity (who does?). Nonetheless, given Lorelai's fierce independence, her lightning-fast, razor-sharp tongue and wit, and her tendency to veer precipitously between strength and vulnerability, Lorelai is a prototypical Katharine Hepburn character, and it's hard to imagine that Sherman-Palladino didn't have Katherine Hepburn as her muse when she created her.

Of course, Amy Sherman-Palladino's love of movies permeates the Gilmore Girls' world. As much as they love to riff on music, TV, and kitsch, it's obvious that movies occupy a special place in Lorelai and Rory's hearts. Again and again in the show, a big pile of old movies and an amazing volume of junk food is shown as the central bonding ritual in their relationship. It must be said, however, that the "golden age" of Hollywood is not usually the era referenced in the show. The Gilmores' film consciousness seems to begin about 1960 (*Mary Poppins*, or thereabout) and peak in the mid-'70s (*The Godfather*, *Pippi Longstocking*), then carry on through the '80s (*Say Anything*) and '90s (*Thelma & Louise*) up to the present. Of course, it makes sense that the show would most often reference films from its main character's (and its key target demographic's) lifetimes. Important exceptions to the above are the films of Audrey Hepburn, particularly the aforementioned *Sabrina*, which have been referenced several times throughout the show's run.

Let's look at some of the other ways that *Gilmore Girls* draws its inspiration from the comedy of the Golden Age of Hollywood.

Screwball Comedy

Certainly, the most palpable Hollywood influence on the *Gilmore Girls* is the "screwball" comedies of the '30s, '40s, and '50s. The screwball was a baseball pitch perfected by New York Giants pitcher Carl Hubbell. Designed to deceive batters, it was a curve ball with an unexpected twist. The screwball comedies were based on inverting social norms. Poor people were smarter and better balanced than the rich, and women, not men, were the ones who drove romantic relationships (yes, these were subversive ideas in the '30s).

Screwball comedies were a product of the Depression, and most of the pure examples of the form were made in the '30s, but the '40s and '50s saw the continued production of comedies with distinctly screwball characteristics, and the form remains strongly influential on modern films as disparate as *There's Something About Mary* and the films of Woody Allen.

Unlike the broad and (cartoonishly) violent slapstick comedies of the silents, the screwball comedies were driven by repartee and social farce. Although the comedy was fast and vigorous, it was also much more intellectual than the slapsticks. Talking pictures were still a new idea, and directors and screenwriters were eager to use lots of words when they told their stories.

The witty exchanges that marked the screwball comedies were heavily influenced by the plays of Noël Coward, as well as by the writings of poet, playwright, and raconteur Dorothy Parker (who would later be honored by Amy Sherman-Palladino as the namesake of her production company).

Coming shortly after the aforementioned Hays Production Code slammed the door on cinematic sin, skin, and smuttiness, the screwball comedies relied on innuendo and tease for their sexiness. Nonetheless, the comedy was distinctly adult in sensibility, reflecting a mature (if discretely veiled) sexuality.

This exchange, from Howard Hawks's *Bringing Up Baby* (1938)—

one of the most verbally adroit of the screwballs—shows some of the twists and turns that would later become a feature in *Gilmore Girls*. Katharine Hepburn's Susan, a socialite and free spirit, is speaking to a psychologist about Cary Grant's David. It's hard to capture the verbal acrobatics of *Bringing Up Baby* in a single short excerpt, but try to keep in mind that Hepburn's character (who's on screen for most of the movie) keeps up this kind of conversational pace pretty much all the time, and leaves everybody in the film as lost as poor Dr. Lehman:

> DR. LEHMAN: You may have heard me lecture...I usually talk about nervous disorders. I am a psychiatrist.
> SUSAN: Oh! Crazy people.
> DR. LEHMAN: We dislike the use of that word. All people who behave strangely are not insane....
> SUSAN: What would you say about a man who follows a girl around?...
> DR. LEHMAN (listening intently): Follows her around?...
> SUSAN: And then when she talks to him he fights with her?
> DR. LEHMAN: Fights with you?...Is the young man your fiancé?
> SUSAN: Oh no, I don't know him. I never even saw him before today. (Blithely) No, he just follows me around and fights with me.
> DR. LEHMAN: Well, the love impulse in men very frequently reveals itself in terms of conflict.
> SUSAN: The love impulse!
> DR. LEHMAN: Without my knowing anything about it, my rough guess would be that he has a fixation on you.

Besides wit and pacing (Hawks is famous as the first director to have actors overlap their dialogue), the script of *Bringing Up Baby* reflects *Gilmore Girls* in that the heroine is usually at least three or four conversational steps ahead of everyone she meets (this is true in many screwball comedies, but it's particularly distinct in *Baby*). The big difference between Lorelai and *Baby*'s Susan is that while Lorelai's quirkiness is her way of being charming, Susan's quirkiness is because she's more than just a little odd (still charming, but not as consciously so).

The beautiful but independent young socialite who rebels against her upbringing is a staple of the screwballs. Most of them don't break away quite as forcibly as Lorelai did—the Depression-era audiences of the screwballs were hungry for the fantasy of wealth and leisure, and while they might appreciate a heroine who would risk her birthright for love, it wouldn't be a happy ending if she actually lost it—but the parallel is obvious. For example, Claudette Colbert's runaway heiress in Frank Capra's classic *It Happened One Night* starts out as an unregenerate brat, but over the course of the movie she grows in maturity, thanks to some actual contact with working-class reality (and the love of a real man, of course).

Small-Town America

Stars Hollow is certainly the most daringly unrealistic element of *Gilmore Girls*. While Chilton Academy or Richard and Emily Gilmore's social circle are determinedly old-fashioned and conservative, Stars Hollow exists in a parallel universe... or at least a time warp. It's straight out of the '40s—and not the war-torn '40s of history, but the pure Platonic ideal of the '40s as seen in the *Saturday Evening Post* covers of Norman Rockwell. Stars Hollow has no chain restaurants (in fact, as far as we have seen it has no fast food), no big-box stores. It also has (let's face it) no black people, other than the racially ambiguous Michel. As far as we can tell, none of the kids in the high school has ever tried an illegal drug of any kind—this is a town where the teenage rockers go to church every Sunday, and a moody underachiever like Jess Mariano can be viewed as a juvenile delinquent. Now, I know that some small towns in New England go a lot further in setting standards to preserve their nostalgic ambience than communities in the Heartland, where I grew up... but seriously, does a town like Stars Hollow exist anywhere in the twenty-first century other than in the paintings of Thomas Kinkade?

In the '40s and '50s, America was fascinated with small-town living. After surviving the Great Depression only to be thrust into the maelstrom of WWII, followed by the long, tense uneasiness of the Cold War, the American Dream crystallized around a neverland vision of small-town America as the embodiment of prosperity, virtue, and serenity.

Not everybody bought whole-heartedly into this myth. Even in the '50s, some writers and directors knew that small towns could be hotbeds of vicious rumor, petty backbiting, and rampant hypocrisy—

melodramas like *Peyton Place* and the films of Douglas Sirk ruthlessly exposed the secret guts of rustic America.

But in the comedies, things tended to be a great deal sweeter. Any evil that did come to Heartland, USA was probably coming in from the big city and was likely to succumb and repent in the light of the sheer blinding virtue of the salt-of-the earth citizens before the final credits rolled.

Today, this sensibility seems like a very conservative idea, but it actually came out of the left. The nineteenth and early twentieth centuries glorified "high society" with its glitter and affluence, but in the wake of WWI, Marxist thought began making inroads among the American intelligentsia. The Marxist paradigm glorified the worker, the common man. Writers and directors turned against wealth and high society (where they actually lived) and began to glorify small working communities (which they probably had driven through or flown over at some point). It's no wonder this vision of rural living was a bit detached from reality.

Frank Capra, for example, really believed in small-town America. Although he grew up in Los Angeles, as the son of Italian immigrants he knew in his heart that the true essence of the American Dream was waiting out there in working-class America. In films like *Mr. Deeds Goes to Town*, *Mr. Smith Goes to Washington*, and *Meet John Doe* he has heroic rural Everymen carrying the torch of the American Dream out of their rural enclaves and back to the decadent economic and intellectual elites of the cities. In perhaps his most famous film, *It's a Wonderful Life*, he shows us a harrowing juxtaposition of the good, innocent, bucolic small town of Bedford Falls with a vision of a ruined Bedford Falls where rampant capitalism has contaminated the town with pollution, poverty, and vice.

While Capra's vision of small-town America certainly influenced Stars Hollow, there's a crucial difference—Capra saw small-town life as good, but he never, ever saw it as "quaint." Some of the people in Capra's towns might have been charming and quirky, but others were dull, and still others were small-minded or vicious. To Capra, that was merely a believable artistic adaptation of the rich tapestry of American life. Frankly, Capra probably would have been horrified by communities like Stars Hollow, which struggle to stay charming so as to be more attractive to tourists. He certainly would have been more strongly drawn to Luke's "live and let live" philosophy than to Taylor's program of economic advancement through ever-increasing winsomeness.

Gilmore Girls wasn't the only TV show developed in the '90s to feature a comedically idealized vision of small-town America. Shows like *Ed, Key West, Picket Fences*, and, perhaps most notably, *Northern Exposure* all were set in similar small-town quasi-utopias.

Whether they come from the '40s or the '90s, appeared on TV or in film, were inspired by socialist utopianism or jaded turn-of-the-millennium nostalgia, one thing always remains true...small-town comedy is the natural environment of the great character actor. The character actor—an actor who specializes in one consistent portrayal of a character who flaunts and basks in his or her own unique eccentricity—was a crucial part of the classic Hollywood comedy aesthetic. A really good character actor could make a fictional town seem as real as Main Street running past the marquee outside the theatre, while at the same time making it seem somewhere sweeter and more wonderful than mundane reality. In the '60s and '70s directors turned away from the character actor in favor of more naturalistic supporting characters, but recently the art of the character actor has gotten a boost from the hour-long dramatic TV comedy, and nobody on TV has a stronger ensemble of quirky and charming supporting characters than *Gilmore Girls*. From *It's a Wonderful Life's* Bert the Cop and Ernie the Cabbie to *Gilmore Girls'* Kirk, Miss Patty, and Taylor, writers and filmmakers through the years always remember that nothing makes the small-town dream come alive more than a strong stable of gifted character actors.

Teenage Romance

The idea of the teenager is a distinctly twentieth-century concept. Prior to that, you were a child until you started work or got married (or, if you were very, very lucky, went to college), at which time you became an adult. The idea of a transitional state between childhood and adulthood didn't even occur to anybody until the industrialized prosperity of the twentieth century gave children (in America, anyway) a few extra years to devote to growing up.

In the '30s, swing music provided the cornerstone of a "youth culture," with fashion, music, and vocabulary quite distinct from the square adults. In the '50s, rock 'n' roll music catapulted the youth culture to a whole new level, while at the same time adult society started to fear that the whole teenage thing was getting out of hand. The term "juvenile delinquency" was coined. (In the '60s, of course, everybody's worst fears were confirmed.)

With the birth of teenage and youth culture, it was only natural that films for and about teens would soon follow.

Of course, teenage comedy (and drama, and horror) are pervasive in modern films and TV shows. But Rory Gilmore's story doesn't seem to fit in very well with fare like *Beverly Hills, 90210* and *The O.C.* Most teenage shows on TV today deal with temptation and sexual awakening. Even more moralistic shows like *7th Heaven* and *Joan of Arcadia* look at their "good kids" largely in terms of the threats and temptations they face.

Rory's world seems a good deal more innocent. It isn't the sanitized, puritanical innocence of '60s sitcoms, but has more of a sense of balance. Rory does have a sexual dimension—in fact, both she and Paris eventually lose their virginities under somewhat less than morally ideal circumstances (Lane, of course, actually manages to hold out until marriage)—but sex or sexuality are never really at the heart of her character.

The central element of Rory's character is that she's always been protected—defended first by her mother, then by her community, and later by her school and her grandparents. The convention in modern film or TV is that a character who's grown up as "sheltered" as Rory has will be unnaturally naïve, timid, and vulnerable—either that, or when she does find freedom she'll go a little bit crazy. However, Rory's upbringing makes her strong. If she is naïve, it's only because she's young and still learning—her more "sophisticated" friends at Chilton and Yale all tend to be less well-prepared for real life than Rory is.

Whatever Amy Sherman-Palladino's politics may be, this is an intrinsically conservative idea—in fact, it's Biblical. The Book of Proverbs advises, "Train up a child in the way he should go, and when he is old he will not depart from it." Rory is protected, but her protectors—most of all Lorelai—never lie to her or prevent her from seeing the world as it is. By the time she's sixteen, at the start of the series, she's allowed unrestrained access to any books or films she likes, and she's already proven herself well able to handle this responsibility. Rory is not being insulated from the real world; she's being prepared for it.

The clearest cinematic antecedent for Rory's story is probably found in the '30s films of Mickey Rooney and Judy Garland. There are some TV precedents from the '50s and '60s—show's like *Life with Father* and *Ozzie and Harriet*—but those shows tend to be about adults who are raising kids, rather than about the kids themselves, and Rory Gilmore is nobody's supporting character. (*Gidget* and *The Patty Duke Show*—which actually focus on teenage girls—are a bit closer to the mark, but they lie outside the scope of this examination.)

From the formidable Mickey Rooney oeuvre, we get the Andy Hardy films, beginning with *A Family Affair* in 1937 and probably best exemplified by *Love Finds Andy Hardy* in 1941. In Hardy's hometown of Carvel we see a clear preview of Stars Hollow. Like Rory, Andy is a good kid from a good family in a good town. He's allowed to make his own mistakes, but when his back is up against the wall he can always rely on his dad, kindly old Judge Hardy to help him find his way. Both Andy Hardy and Rory Gilmore are shown earnestly taking on a series of none-too-earth-shattering dilemmas, while a nurturing safety-net of loving adults stands nearby, letting the kids make their own way but always ready to rally to their support before things can get too bad. Andy Hardy had his very nuclear family at his back, while it takes the village of Stars Hollow to raise Rory Gilmore, but either way it's a similarly charming and comforting fantasy of a safe and loving upbringing.

In our imaginary *Gilmore Girls* movie we cast Audrey Hepburn as Rory. This makes sense for chronological reasons, and because of the definite resemblance between Hepburn and Alexis Bledel, but perhaps the actress who best embodies the spirit of Rory Gilmore is Mickey Rooney's frequent co-star, the young Judy Garland. Like Rory, the teenage Judy in most of her films is innocent but grounded, compassionate but clear-eyed, uncommonly gifted, pragmatic, and always willing to take on a challenge. Judy could organize the local kids to turn her uncle's old barn into a venue for a Busby Berkeley-sized singing and dancing spectacular with the same élan that Rory would later display in preparing a business plan with Paris for econ class or organizing a DAR fundraiser for her grandmother.

The Miracle of Morgan's Creek

In closing, let's look at one film comedy that brings together all of the elements we've looked at so far: *The Miracle of Morgan's Creek* (1944) by Preston Sturges.

Preston Sturges started out as a screenwriter and became probably the last great director of the screwball comedy era. Sturges was much more a satirist than his compatriots Hawks and Capra. He's perhaps best remembered for *Sullivan's Travels* (1941), starring Joel McCrea and Veronica Lake—a penetrating satire of Hollywood and its relationship to the real American culture in the waning days of the Great Depression.

The Miracle of Morgan's Creek is an even more biting social satire. It tells the story of Trudy Kockenlocker (the high school locker-room quality of the character's last name is probably not at all accidental), played by Betty Hutton. Trudy, the respectable and perky daughter of the town constable, considers it her patriotic duty to entertain the soldiers who pass through town on their way to deployment overseas. But one night the entertainment gets a little out of hand, and Trudy wakes up the next morning married and pregnant. Her new husband has shipped out, and Trudy has no clear idea who he is. With the help of a local boy who's had a secret crush on Trudy for years, she sets out to find her baby's father. Hi-jinks, as they are wont to do, ensue.

There are obvious echoes between Trudy's story and the story of the young Lorelai Gilmore. In addition, we have the wit and pacing of screwball comedy, as well as the upending of social mores. We have a small town inhabited by memorable character actors, and we have teenagers learning about life. The biggest difference between *Gilmore Girls* and *The Miracle of Morgan's Creek* is that, in its own wartime way, *Morgan's Creek* is actually the edgier of the two. Sturges was a satirist, and as such, he has his heroine's dilemma grow precipitously throughout the movie—well before the end of the movie, the governor is taking a personal hand in the search for Trudy's lost husband. Because of the Hays Code, Sturges couldn't have Trudy just go out, get drunk, and get knocked up. Instead, Sturges goes to preposterous lengths to keep his screenplay morally correct. Contrary to all logic, Trudy is duly wedded before she is bedded, and her inconvenient loss of memory comes from an ill-timed knock on the head rather than an alcoholic fog. Sturges makes the setup to Trudy's predicament so absurd that he's actually mocking the Production Code in complying with it. Furthermore, Trudy's scandalized hometown is neither as lovable nor as loving as Stars Hollow, and Trudy (whom you may have guessed by now is a bit of an air-head) could never have been played by Judy Garland or either of the Hepburns.

It's interesting that the one film that comes the closest to the *Gilmore Girls* in overall theme and tone is one of the last and most cynical of the screwball comedies. No matter how modern it may often seem, *Gilmore Girls* actually hearkens back to Golden Age Hollywood innocence other similar shows can't quite achieve. But there's something remaining about Golden Age Hollywood romantic comedy that we can point to, and maybe even evoke, but never really recapture, even with *Gilmore Girls*. Maybe it's not worth trying; we've come a long way since then, to a place where no one bats an eye at a Lane or a Michel. Still, if you're looking for evidence that *Gilmore Girls* was created to try to recapture the spirit of the classic Hollywood comedy, *The Miracle of Morgan's Creek* is an excellent place to start your search.

> **Chris McCubbin** has written more than twenty books, mostly about games (computer and otherwise). He's a co-founder of and writer/editor with Incan Monkey God Studios. Chris lives in Austin, Texas, with his wife, Lynette Alcorn, and his dogs, Penny and Sammy.

References

A Family Affair. dir. George B. Seitz. Perf. Lionel Barrymore, Mickey Rooney. Metro-Goldwyn-Mayer, 1937.

Bringing Up Baby. dir. Howard Hawks. Perf. Katherine Hepburn, Cary Grant. RKO Radio Pictures, 1938.

It's a Wonderful Life. dir. Frank Capra. Perf. James Stewart, Donna Reed. Liberty Films, Inc., 1946.

Love Finds Andy Hardy. dir. George B. Seitz. Perf. Mickey Rooney, Judy Garland, Lewis Stone. Metro-Goldwyn-Mayer, 1938.

Sabrina. dir. Billy Wilder. Perf. Audrey Hepburn. Paramount Pictures, 1954.

The Miracle at Morgan's Creek. dir. Preston Sturges. Perf. Betty Hutton, Eddie Bracken. Paramount Pictures, 1944.

Carol Cooper

"Mama Don't Preach"
Class, Culture, and Lorelai Gilmore as Bizarro-World Suffragette

KIRK: Your choice is unorthodox.
LORELAI: That's because I'm not orthodox. I'm liberal with a touch
of reform and a smidgen of *zippity-pow!* ("Just Like Gwen and
Gavin," 6-12)

Lorelai Gilmore does everything backward (if not in high heels), Carol
Cooper says, making choices so inexplicable she must be part of Bizarro World. Then you look closer at Lorelai's choices and they're not
so much bizarre as bold.

THE TELEVISION CHARACTER of Lorelai Gilmore is bright,
pretty, funny, entrepreneurial, and a man-magnet. So why
might the average girl viewer—perhaps already a fan of Beyoncé or Gwen Stefani—shy away from Lorelai Gilmore as
a positive role model? Maybe it's because she does everything backwards, like the denizens of Bizarro World, Superman's loopy alternate
universe. The whole premise of Lorelai's saga is that (like Bizarro Lois
Lane) Lorelai does the opposite of what more conventional or prudent modern women would do. And yet she survives and thrives on
the decidedly mixed results.

Lorelai has unprotected sex when she shouldn't; gets pregnant then
decides neither to marry nor get rid of the child; abandons a background of wealth for blue-collar poverty; and postpones college for
subsistence toil and single parenthood. Not the most practical or glam-

orous life choices in the world. But what makes Lorelai worth respecting as an unconventional heroine is her refusal to let questionable choices defeat or define her. As surreal as a fish on a bicycle, Lorelai serves as an object lesson for distaff America on how to triumph over bad luck (since she can't seem to avoid it). You can almost hear her Bizarro war cry: "Freedom and privilege? Lorelai *hate* freedom and privilege. Me rather prove me am tough and independent by trading youth for more hard work and responsibility than me can handle! Lorelai not spoiled, me am liberated!" And by the standards of her own internal logic, this contrarian suffragette is absolutely right.

American feminists only had thirteen years to revel in the Supreme Court's decision regarding *Roe v. Wade* before Madonna—up 'til then a veritable poster-child for sexual freedom and planned parenthood—released a hit single in 1986 which suggested that some young women might have to fight society as fiercely to *keep* their unplanned pregnancies as others had to fight for the legal right to terminate them. This perspective on the abortion option wasn't new, but it certainly wasn't a fashionable viewpoint in the liberal media of those times. So in the fall of 2000, when a new television show dared to explore the long-term results of the "pro-life" choice of an upper-class teen (who could have lost her cherry to "Papa Don't Preach" on the car radio), Americans were once again asked to re-define our freedoms and our cost-versus-benefit lifestyles from a Second-Wave Feminist perspective.

The genius of *Gilmore Girls* is that it's about class, it's about small towns, it's about Eastern Establishment snobbery, it's about gender options, it's about single-parent households, *and* it's about mother-daughter relationships. Strangely, it all but ignores race. The racial issues are oddly skewed because the population of mythological Stars Hollow comprises mainly iconic white ethnics and just one Asian family—a New World Order demographic prefigured in *The Simpsons* and *King of the Hill*. Such token ethnic representation is ordinarily used to make even the quirkiest white protagonist seem relatively "normal," even allowing them to appear racially unbiased because non-whites are not numerous enough to be seen as significant threats or competition. But on *Gilmore Girls*, racial and ethnic tokenism is a narrative decoy that permits deeper explorations of American class anxieties.

For example, Lorelai's coworker Michel is a weirdly effeminate black Francophone male whose judgmental, superior attitude implies that bitchy egotism has neither color nor gender. Here he also functions as a status-seeking stand-in for every black character the show doesn't include—plus every gay, big city, cosmopolitan or aggressive immigrant striver it chooses to exclude—all while being conveniently off-limits as a potential sex-object for Lorelai. Mrs. Kim, dictatorial mother of Rory's Korean best friend Lane, uses her fanatic involvement in evangelical Christianity to elevate her status and opinions above those of lumpen Stars Hollow residents. But almost every denizen of Stars Hollow is shown being more aggressive about proving and defending some sort of pride in social position than Lorelai. Having already found the obligations of being born into "high society" somewhat hollow, she refuses to fall back into the trap of allowing her self-worth to be externally defined.

Sure, she works hard and goes to business school to improve herself, but it's clear she does these things more for self-satisfaction than to score points with the world at large. The maverick drummer Lorelai marches to plays a distinctively Bohemian beat, freeing her from the lock-step moves needed to "keep up" with the middle and upper classes. Considering that Lorelai, likely intentionally, mirrors the public face of feminism in the U.S. (which has always been predominantly white and middle class) this abdication of classist priorities is a welcome but suspicious innovation. Can anyone who has tasted the advantages of rank honestly renounce them forever? It's little wonder that her character provokes some derisive eye-rolling among involuntarily poor multi-ethnic single mothers. But it's precisely the fairy-tale fantasy elements in Lorelai's story that makes it so subversively entertaining.

Most contemporary "dramedies" display more mean-spirited and self-destructive interactions between key characters than *Gilmore Girls* does. Theirs is a far more genteel sort of dysfunctionality than previously made popular by *The Simpsons* or *Roseanne*, or *Married...with Children*. This is part of why this program sidelines most racial issues and disputes. The focus here is the feckless journey of Lorelai Gilmore through a picaresque world as improbably benign as possible. It helps that the show's youthful stars are cast as lovable, lighthearted madcaps. No brooding, bitter, nascent sociopaths here to break the spell of the show's blithe, yet oddly relentless, optimism. And yet what a change from the *Donna Reed/Leave It to Beaver/7th Heaven* model of suburban familyhood! Even paradigm-shifting programs like *All in the Family* and *Married...with Children* are not as different as *Gilmore Girls* in its central premise. An unwed mother had never been the narrative pivot of a hit TV show before. So this program, which celebrates a "disgraced" Connecticut Brahmin teen heiress who flees prep school to keep and raise her now-teenaged daughter while estranged from her own parents, remains a huge twist on tried-and-true television formulas.

When we first met Lorelai Gilmore, she was the thirty-something mom of a delightful young high school student who was nearly the same age Lorelai was when she gave birth. Up until then no adolescent rebellion had taken place, so mother and daughter were still so close that Lorelai had yet to imagine her daughter Rory as a separate human being. Instead, she increasingly saw Rory as a mirror image of herself at that age, and consequently began to relive her own fears and regrets about past choices and past temptations. Although proud of having stood up to her rich parents and created a life for herself and her child without their help, she found herself suddenly wanting to offer her kid all the upper-class benefits that she abandoned and therefore could no longer afford. So *Gilmore Girls* doesn't only reexamine feminist prerogatives, but also the importance of class, gender, regional culture, and social pressure in shaping female destinies.

Set somewhere in New England in as unbelievably bucolic a town as Andy Griffith's Mayberry (replete with ditzy surrogates for goofy Goober Pyle, meddlesome Aunt Bee, and manic Barney Fife), the tale of Lorelai Gilmore and her cheerfully illegitimate daughter unfolds both as a critique of inbred Eastern Establishment conventionality and as a kind of reverse negative of Mayberry's quaint Southern squirreliness.[1] Skewering these time-honored stereotypes of Anglo-American normalcy, *Gilmore Girls* further subverts the classic formula for televised family drama by giving star-billing to an unwed mother who is not stigmatized for her choices.

---

[1] Hollywood portrayed the supporting cast of *The Andy Griffith Show* as a collection of eccentrics and laconic goofballs, all mildly stereotyped along the lines of Yankee preconceptions about Southern/hillbilly clichés. It's interesting to see the residents of Stars Hollow and Lorelai's upper crust parents being similarly exaggerated and burlesqued according to the provincial Yankee myths and stereotypes, implying that "north" and "south" are not so different when it comes to inbred regional habits.

It wasn't that television hadn't dealt with wise, funny, beloved single parents before, even giving them leading roles in *The Andy Griffith Show*, *My Three Sons*, *Julia*, and *The Courtship of Eddie's Father*, to name a few. But these lead characters could be single only if the lead character's spouse was lost by divorce, death, or post-marriage abandonment. The Gilmore story flips this script in ways that question what women have come to expect from "liberation" in the past twenty years. Women who value career and personal freedom above all might wonder why a post *Roe v. Wade* high school debutante from "old line" money would refuse the obvious options of (1) abortion; (2) shotgun—but not obligatorily permanent—wedding to the "nice boy from a good family" who knocked her up; or (3) intra- or extra-family adoption, to run away from home and raise her child by the blue-collar sweat of her own brow. Lorelai not only gave up material comfort for motherhood—she passed up college, travel, upscale friends, leisure time, and a disposable income. The first question viewers are forced to ask (and every episode strives to answer) is: *Was it worth it?*

From the very first episode of the first season we have seen the depth of Lorelai's rapport with her daughter Rory: they finish each other's sentences, they have the same irreverent wit, the same easy affection for people, the same love for old movies, comfort food, and obscure pop culture references. In short, this is the most idealized mother-daughter relationship on earth. Men come and go—but these two hang tough. They are so seamlessly bonded that suddenly you know where Lorelai poured the energy she might otherwise have invested in college life, high society, or in conforming to her own parents' expectations. Ironically, what most endangers this bond is a lingering class anxiety: Lorelai's desire to guarantee her child opportunities Lorelai missed.

When Rory gets a chance to leave her small-town public high school for a prestigious prep school, Lorelai has to sacrifice their hard-won independence from her parents to pay for it. Mandatory weekly dinners with the elder Gilmores follow in which Lorelai finds herself strangely ambivalent about watching her daughter slowly seduced by the set of class values Lorelai once happily left behind. Interestingly enough, Lorelai's reflective ambivalence about her privileged origins—and the roads necessarily not taken—transforms her (philosophically speaking) into a rich, matriarchal WASP version of a Buddhist renunciate.

To follow the analogy you must see that Lorelai has given up the comforts of home and inherited wealth to raise her daughter outside of the "illusory" materialistic value system of her parents. She has invented her own philosophy of Positive Parenting, and sought the hard-won freedom of Self-Empowerment. But instead of achieving true liberation from dependence on her parents' world, she has kept one foot in Samsara, not realizing that wanting her daughter to have the same perks she herself once rejected means she is still invested in their value system. Read this way, as a Buddhist parable, the relationship between Lorelai and Rory is doomed to deteriorate as soon as we locate the remnants of Lorelai's ego in her projections of her own wants and fears onto her daughter. For these egotistical projections are what eventually cause the same problems (issues of control and lifestyle[2]) between Lorelai and her kid that initially manifested between Lorelai and her own mother many years before. It takes awhile for our heroine to figure all this out, and in the interim she and Rory suffer through a few long, predictably painful disagreements about the pursuit of happiness.

Another way the show illuminates class and cultural anxiety is through Lane Kim, Rory's oldest and best friend, who has mother problems of her own. Functioning as a Korean doppelgänger of Rory, Lane is the only daughter of an antique-store owning, evangelical Christian matriarch who left Korea in part to escape a domineering Buddhist mother (according to "I Get a Sidekick Out of You," 6-19). Juxtaposed against the multigenerational mama-drama of the Gilmores, the Kims provide a narrative excuse to more deeply question why cultural and class "slippage" still looms as so large a threat to most American families. Mrs. Kim fears Rory is a bad influence on Lane because of the downward mobility Lorelai represents. Since only wacky Bohemians get to *choose* what class they belong to (as Lorelai has), Mrs. Kim imagines the younger as spreading a Bohemian contagion to Lane by example. So it's no surprise that Lorelai's mom bonds

---

[2] Does Lorelai really want to force her daughter to live according to Lorelai's tastes and rules? Is she so egotistical that she thinks she has the right to impose her ideas and lifestyle choices onto anyone else, including her own daughter? Where does a mother end and a daughter begin? These are the same unreconciled problems that drove a wedge between Lorelai and her own mom.

instantly with not just Michel but also Mrs. Kim the first time she meets them. She instinctively gravitates towards the only two people in town as critical of Lorelai as she is, and whose attachment to class boundaries rivals her own.

To some extent Lorelai must agree with them, because she urges Rory to go to prep school despite the fact that she is already getting A's in public high school. Moreover, by "The Road Trip to Harvard" (2-4), we see that being manager of a local inn is only the beginning of Lorelai's entrepreneurial aspirations—it's clear that she genuinely desires upward mobility for herself as well as her daughter. But unlike her parents, Lorelai craves an upward mobility free of proprietary entitlement issues, and on her own terms.

In partnering with her best friend and co-worker to buy their own inn, Lorelai shows initiative inherited from Mia, the owner of her existing workplace, who hired and mentored Lorelai when she first left home with baby Rory. A confrontation during "The Ins and Outs of Inns" (2-8) between Lorelai's mom and Mia revealed that Emily resents the years her child and grandchild spent under Mia's protective tutelage. But those misgivings come less from the resulting loss of familial memories than because it gave Lorelai the working-class skills to escape inherited class obligations and to make her own way in the world. That's one reason why Lorelai is powerful and fearless in ways Mrs. Kim and Mrs. Gilmore are not. She's self-confident enough to accept those things she can't control and to rely upon the kindness of strangers. Class anxieties generally arise from the idea that neither individuals nor families can prosper without vast, mutually obligated social networks. Whether women marry into a preferred class or work their way into one, binding themselves to the consequent web of in-group obligations can seem the best way to control their environment. Yet, as both Mrs. Kim and Mrs. Gilmore discover, the compulsive need for control creates paranoia and oppression, not security. People may need networks to survive, and yes, economic and cultural ties help form them. But to really thrive people need flexibility, self-confidence, and emotional generosity even more.

By the time Lorelai has her own business up and running (via business classes and a timely loan), Rory is already established at Yale, and both women have nursed each another through romantic disasters that say as much about the impossible feminist goal of "having it all" as about the craft of compromise which modern women still find difficult to master. Mrs. Kim hopes to spare her daughter the chaos of shopping for male companionship by hours of asexual worship in church and carefully chosen and chaperoned "dates." But her best efforts are doomed to fail, for despite wealth, brains, breeding, or religion, every would-be superwoman in the *Gilmore Girls* universe reacts to romance as a form of Kryptonite. In fact, *Gilmore Girls* is so much about relationships between strong women that all the male characters—whether boyfriends, husbands, colleagues, or fathers—seem a bit weak and somehow disappointing by comparison. And yet, come hell or high water, these girls've gotta have 'em! It's not that any of them think they *need* a man to be successful in life. They just can't resist attempting the fantasy of perfection successful couplehood might bring.

It was in fact the loss of yet another aspiring suitor over her mother's unreasonable demands that trigged Lane's first open act of defiance. She had to be drunk to do it, but once she declared her determination to have her rock band and her Anglo boyfriends too, Lane started a process of emancipation, separation, and reconciliation that ultimately culminated in Mrs. Kim helping book her daughter's band and allowing her to marry a white band mate. Part of why Mrs. Kim was able to change relatively quickly compared to Emily Gilmore comes down to differences in culture and class. First, as a working woman and head of her household, Mrs. Kim is more pragmatic than Emily ever had to be. Second, as an Asian immigrant to the U.S., she has already adapted to bigger adjustments and compromises than this. Resisting additional change was what seemed appropriate at first, but seeing her daughter struggle and sacrifice for what she believes in —after knowing the history of Emily, Lorelai, and Rory—won her respect and support in the end.

Compared to Lane and the machinations involved in her struggle to live on her own terms, Rory has clearly won the mom lottery here. Thanks to the legality of *Roe v. Wade*, she never has to question why she was brought into the world. She wasn't born to measure up to some imaginary family legacy, nor was she produced as a tax write-off, free labor, or an afterthought. Even when they disagree, as happens more and more often as the series progresses, the foundation of mutual respect Lorelai and Rory have for each other allows them to avoid the deep and possibly permanent damage suffered by less compassionate and less self-aware mother/daughter dyads.

As the object of a loving (if slightly manipulative) tug of war between her rich, well-connected grandparents, and her self-reliant, fiercely devoted mother, Rory clearly has all the genetic and material resources she needs to become whoever she wants or needs to be. After all, she is the scion of a true twenty-first century anomaly: the contrarian, Bizarro-World suffragette. Lorelai Gilmore: the girl who, when faced with a plethora of pro-choice, haute-Feminist (and some would say even more appealing) options, decided that choosing to leave home alone to have her baby was the healthier, more revolutionary, liberating, and self-affirming thing to do.

Carol Cooper is a New York-based journalist and cultural critic who has been writing professionally about books, music, film, pop trends, and social issues for more than twenty years. Her work has been published in various national and international publications, including *Essence*, *Elle*, *Latin N.Y.*, *The Face* (England), *Actuel* (France), the *Village Voice*, the *New York Times*, and *Rolling Stone*. Her work has been cited in academic journals, and her critical and sociological essays have been included in a number of anthologies, including *Rolling Stone: The '70s* (Little, Brown and Company), *Brooklyn: A State of Mind* (Workman Publishing Company), *Dark Matter 2: Reading the Bones* (Warner Aspect), and *The Rolling Stone Book of Women in Rock* (Random House). In December of 2006 she published a hardcover anthology assessing the most significant cultural trends from the closing decades of the twentieth century in an essay collection from Nega Fulo Books called *Pop Culture Considered as an Uphill Bicycle Race: Selected Critical essays 1979 to 2001*. She is a member of the national nonprofit comics advocacy group Friends of Lulu and a 1974 graduate of the Clarion Writer's Workshop for Fantasy and Science Fiction. She is widely traveled and holds both B.A. and M.A.L.S. degrees from Wesleyan University in Connecticut.

Coffee at Luke's-*isms*

W**HAT WOULD AN ANTHOLOGY** about *Gilmore Girls* be without an addendum explaining all the high-brow and low-brow cultural references used in the book? It's like the little season-by-season DVD booklets, but harder to lose.

7ᵗʰ Heaven—WB television series about a minister's family in California that began in 1996. Though its series finale was in 2006, it was renewed for yet another season when the WB merged with UPN to create the CW.

The actor became Alexis Bledel's real boyfriend off the show—Reference to Milo Ventimiglia, who played Luke Danes's troubled nephew Jess on *Gilmore Girls* and went on to star in the NBC show *Heroes*. He and Bledel dated for more than three years before breaking up.

Jenny: Probably because he got tired of having complete strangers yell, "We liked Cute Dean better!" whenever they were together.

Agnes Moorehead—Oscar-nominated character actress best known for her role as Endora in *Bewitched*, and for bringing eyelash-to-eyebrow blue eye shadow to primetime.

Jenny: The spiritual role model for Emily Gilmore.

Alias—ABC series that ran from 2001 to 2006. Created by J. J. Abrams and starring Jennifer Garner, it focused on Garner as Sydney Bristow, a kick-ass spy who changed her hair color a lot.

All in the Family—1971–1979 CBS sitcom about bigoted Archie Bunker and his good-hearted wife, Edith. The show pushed the television envelope by talking about controversial topics such as homosexuality and racism.

Ally McBeal—FOX television series that ran from 1997 to 2002 and starred Calista Flockhart as a young, single lawyer trying to find love and happiness.

*Jenny: And a cookie. FOX's contribution to anorexia, the anti-*Gilmore Girls, *since Lorelai and Rory never stop eating*

Alvy Moore—Actor best known for playing the friendly but forgetful county agent Hank Kimball on the 1960s sitcom *Green Acres.*

The Andy Griffith Show—Television series that ran on CBS from 1960 to 1968 and was based on the life of the widowed Sheriff Andy Taylor, his small son Opie, and the other quirky characters that populated the town of Mayberry.

Andy Hardy—Character played by Mickey Rooney in fifteen MGM films from 1937 to 1947. The film franchise grew with Andy, taking him from a carefree boy to a WWII vet.

Andrea Dworkin—Radical feminist who in the 1970s and '80s gained fame for her outspokenness against pornography on the grounds that it led to rape and other violence. She also authored ten books on feminist theory.

Anthony Comstock—Politician and postal inspector in the Victorian era who was dedicated to preserving morality. He fought against pornography and birth control.

The Apostle Paul's letter to the Philippians—Letter to the church of Philippi spreading the gospel, written by Paul while he was imprisoned.

Asaad Kelada—Television director that Kirk confused with legendary Japanese film director Akira Kurasawa when citing his own influences in the making of *A Short Film by Kirk.*

Audrey Hepburn—Iconic film actress who spent her later years working as an ambassador for UNICEF, and who is still considered a fashion and beauty icon. Starred in such pictures as *Breakfast at Tiffany's, Sabrina,* and *My Fair Lady.*

Aunt Bee—Andy Taylor's aunt and housekeeper in *The Andy Griffith Show,* who helped Andy raise his son Opie.

Barbara Bush—Wife of former President George H. W. Bush and First Lady from 1989 to 1993. She was devoted to literacy and other worthy causes.

Jenny: Maybe, but she's still on my list for calling Hillary a "rhymes with witch." Just say it, Barbara.

Barney Fife—Deputy sheriff of Mayberry in *The Andy Griffith Show*. Though he was eager to enforce the law he was also a perpetual bungler; his name is synonymous with someone enthusiastic but incompetent.

Jenny: Although falling out of use now in favor of the more popular "Kirk."

Bella Abzug—Outspoken New York City congresswoman and women's rights activist from the 1970s.

Benito Mussolini—Reviled fascist dictator of Italy from 1922–1943.

Jenny: But he did make the trains run on time. Bring him back and put him in charge of O'Hare, that's what I say.

Bernard Goetz—"Subway Vigilante" who shot four men during an attempted robbery on a NYC #2 train and then was acquitted on the grounds of self-defense.

Beverly Hills, 90210—FOX primetime soap that ran from 1990 to 2000 that followed the lives of privileged teens and became one of Fox's top shows, making its teen idols household names.

Beverly Hills, Capeside Mass, the O.C.—Locations for the popular teen-focused television series *Beverly Hills, 90120, Dawson's Creek*, and *The O.C.*

Big and Little Edie…at old Grey Gardens—Reference to the cult-favorite 1975 documentary about the eccentric aunt and cousin of Jacqueline Kennedy Onassis, Edith Bouvier Beale (Big Edie), and her daughter (Little Edie), who lived in a crumbling mansion called Grey Gardens in East Hampton, New York.

Jenny: And my absolute favorite allusion in this whole anthology.

Book of Proverbs—Book from the Old Testament that teaches wisdom and virtue through the use of parables.

Jenny: Sort of the way Lorelai and Rory teach wisdom through the use of allusions to Elvis and the Barefoot Contessa.

Boomer—Reference to a "baby boomer," someone who was born between WWII and the start of the Vietnam War.

Boston Brahmins—Wealthy social class of New Englanders who can trace their lineage back to the founders of the city of Boston, Massachusetts. In Hindi Brahmin means "Purest Person."

Bringing Up Baby—1938 screwball comedy directed by Howard Hawks and starring Katharine Hepburn and Cary Grant. The film flopped at the time but is now considered to be one of the best in the genre.

Buffy the Vampire Slayer—Cult TV show that ran from 1997 to 2003, on the WB and then UPN, about the struggles of Buffy Summers, played by Sarah Michelle Gellar, to save the world from the forces of evil.

Jenny: It wasn't so much a cult as a group of extremely sophisticated viewers who appreciated the deep structure of the narratives and the well-wrought metaphorical implications there-in. And I have two Spike action figures to prove it.

Busby-Berkeley-sized singing and dancing spectacular—Reference to the huge song and dance numbers Berkeley choreographed in the 1930s using scores of showgirls filmed from above in complex kaleidoscope-like geometric patterns.

Cary Grant—Quintessential suave film star of the twentieth century who starred in movies such as *The Philadelphia Story* and *Bringing Up Baby*. His name has become synonymous with good looks, good manners, and good humor.

Jenny: I don't care if he is dead, every time I see His Girl Friday, *I still want to have his baby.*

Charles Emerson Winchester III (*M*A*S*H*)—Supporting character in *M*A*S*H*. Winchester was from a wealthy and aristocratic Boston family and on his way to becoming a respected surgeon when he was drafted into the Korean War.

Jenny: Which leads to the question, how wealthy were they if they couldn't get him out of the draft?

Charlie Chan—Chinese-American detective who first appeared in books before moving on to radio, film, a comic strip, and even board games. The films have been criticized because the character was portrayed by white actors rather than Asians.

Jenny: If you go back and read the books, they're not exactly master-pieces of enlightenment, either, Number One Son.

Claudette Colbert—French-American actress who won an Academy Award for *It Happened One Night.* She was one of the most popular actresses of her time, starring in sixty-seven films.

Jenny: That scene where she stops the truck by pulling up her skirt: brilliant. And I don't care if they take away my NOW card for saying it.

Cliff Robertson—Actor who won the 1968 Best Actor Oscar for *Charly.* He also starred in more than seventy other films.

Club hopping together like Lindsay Lohan and her mom—Reference to ex-Disney starlet Lohan's party-girl lifestyle and her mother's tendency to follow along to keep an eye on her.

Jenny: Which, tragically, she has stopped doing. Come back, Dina, and bring underwear for Britney.

Condi Rice—Condoleezza Rice, Secretary of State under President George W. Bush, after whom Kirk modeled a hand-carved mailbox.

Jenny: Genius. Sheer genius.

The Courtship of Eddie's Father—1970s television series based on the movie of the same name, which revolved around a single father trying to raise his son while also finding love.

Don Quixote—Hero of Miguel de Cervantes Saavedra's Spanish novel *Don Quixote de la Mancha.* Quixote is an idealistic but insane man who falsely believes that he is a knight and journeys out on a quest to do good.

Dorothy Parker—American writer and poet who used her sharp wit to criticize twentieth-century society. She was also admired by Amy Sherman-Palladino, who named her production company "Dorothy Parker Drank Here."

Jenny: She is also admired by Jenny Crusie, who often cites her as a major influence.

Douglas Sirk—German-born film director who helmed the hit movies *Magnificent Obsession* and *Imitation of Life*. His American film career spanned from the 1930s to the 1950s.

Eastern Establishment—Socially and financially dominant network of elite universities, institutions, and families of the northeastern United States.

Jenny: Sort of like the French in a Monty Python movie.

East Village—Neighborhood in Manhattan often linked to arts and culture.

Jenny: Until the housing values went insane, and arts and culture had to move to Hoboken to afford the rents.

Ed—2000–2004 NBC series about a lawyer who moved to small-town Ohio after his big city life fell apart, and set up his own law firm in a bowling alley.

Jenny: People thought this was quirky, but in Ohio, bowling alleys have the best food. Plus that's where all the foot traffic is. Ed was a genius.

Edmund Gwenn—Veteran of more than eighty films who played Kris Kringle in 1947's *Miracle on 34th Street*. Playwright George Bernard Shaw personally cast him in several of his plays.

Entertainment Weekly magazine—Publication focused on entertainment media such as films, music, TV shows, etc.

Jenny: Could somebody tell them to quit reviewing my books as chick lit? Thank you.

Epaphroditus—Companion of the apostle Paul who so devoted himself to his missionary work that he became very ill and almost died.

A Family Affair—First Andy Hardy film, released in 1937.

Family Friendly Programming Forum—Organization of more than forty advertisers whose goal is to increase family friendly television. The shows it advocates have to appeal to and be appropriate for different generations, and resolve conflicts responsibly.

Jenny: You know, just like your family does.

The films of Woody Allen—Diverse body of work by prolific writer, actor, and director who often casts himself in his own films.

His works include *Annie Hall, Manhattan,* and *Hannah and Her Sisters.*

Jenny: Not to mention Mia and Her Daughter. Well, it's the elephant in the living room; let's say howdy.

The Financial Times—Business newspaper distinguished not only by its content but by the pink paper it's printed on.

Jenny: If a woman's group did that, there would be comments and snickers. I'm just saying.

Foghorn Leghorn and the baby chicken hawk—Warner Brothers' cartoon characters that are often at odds with one another.

Frasier Crane (*Cheers, Frasier*)—Secondary *Cheers* character who received his own long-running spin-off. Crane was an intellectual radio psychologist from an upper-class background who was often snobbish and reserved.

Frank Capra—Classic American director who produced many popular films in the 1930s and '40s, including *Mr. Deeds Goes to Town, Mr. Smith Goes to Washington,* and the perennial holiday favorite *It's a Wonderful Life.*

Gidget—1950s and '60s teen who loved sand, sun, and surfing. The character was adapted from a novel for several movies and a television show starring the perky Sally Field.

Jenny: I bet she loves being called "perky."

Gloria Steinem—Feminist icon who started her career as a journalist in the 1960s, founded *Ms. Magazine,* and went on to become one of the most recognizable faces of the movement.

Golden Age of Hollywood—Hollywood era characterized by the rise of the studio system and spanning the years from the start of "talkies" in 1927 through the 1940s. Most films produced during this period fell into the categories of Westerns, comedies, film noir, musicals, and biopics.

Gomer Pyle—Character on *The Andy Griffith Show* who worked at the Mayberry filling station first as an attendant and then a mechanic. His character later left the show to join the United States Marine Corps.

Jenny: The few, the proud, the spun-off.

Goober Pyle—Character on *The Andy Griffith Show* who replaced his cousin Gomer as mechanic at the filling station.

Gore Vidal—Prolific American writer of novels, plays, and essays famous for his wit and outspoken opinions, who ran for Congress in the 1960s.

Harold Peary—Distinctive voice actor best known from the radio, television, and film comedies *The Great Gildersleeve*.

Hiltons—Refers to the Hilton Hotel family, which includes celebutante sisters Paris and Nicky.

Hugh Jackman in a white leisure suit—Reference to Jackman's starring role in *The Boy from Oz*, a Broadway musical about the life of the Australian singer/songwriter Peter Allen.

I'm With the Band—Memoir by Pamela Des Barres, a famous groupie in the 1960s and '70s who had affairs with Mick Jagger, Jim Morrison, and other rock stars.

Infuriating teenage gabfest—Reference to the CW's "Aerie Girls," whose comments followed every episode of *Gilmore Girls* and *Veronica Mars* during the 2006–2007 television season.

It Happened One Night—1934 screwball romantic comedy directed by Frank Capra and starring Claudette Colbert and Clark Gable. The first film to win all five major Academy Awards.

It's a Wonderful Life—classic 1946 film directed by Frank Capra and starring Jimmy Stewart. After George Bailey contemplates suicide to save his family from financial ruin, his guardian angel appears to show him that his life matters.

James Dean—1960s bad boy movie idol and sex symbol who tragically died young in a car wreck. He starred in such films as *Rebel Without a Cause* and *Giant*.

Joan and Melissa Rivers—Mother and daughter duo who work red carpet shows together and deliver fashion commentary.

Jenny: At least Melissa still has expressions.

Joan of Arcadia—CBS show that aired from 2003 to 2005 featuring a teenage girl who could see and speak to God. Its cancellation was controversial and caused an uproar from fans.

Jenny: God wasn't happy, either.

Joel McCrea—Handsome leading man from the 1930s and '40s who starred in dramas, comedies, and Westerns, such as *Foreign Correspondent* and *Sullivan's Travels*.

John Lennon and the Julian vs. Sean saga—Reference to the rivalry between Lennon's sons, Julian and Sean. John spent more time with and had a better relationship with his and Yoko's son, Sean, which his son from his first marriage, Julian, resented.

Jenny: Plus Sean got a Playstation and Julian totally didn't.

Julia—1960s television series aired on NBC about a widowed single mother. The program was considered groundbreaking at the time for its portrayal of African-American women in a non-stereotypical way.

Julian Schnabel—New York City artist and filmmaker famous for his neo-expressionist "plate paintings"—paintings done on canvases of broken ceramic plates—and for directing the film *Basquiat*.

Katharine Hepburn—Independent, outspoken actress who starred in such pictures as *The Philadelphia Story* and *The African Queen*, had a decades-long relationship with Spencer Tracy, and made menswear fashionable before its time.

Kathleen Freeman—Character actress in film, stage, and television whose career spanned more than fifty years, from the 1940s until her death in 2001. Freeman had regular or recurring roles in many sitcoms and films series including Peg's mom on *Married...with Children*.

Key West—Short-lived 1993 FOX series about a factory worker who became wealthy and moved to the small town of Key West to try his hand at writing, finding inspiration in the exploits of his quirky neighbors.

Kim Jong Il—The leader of North Korea about whom little is known. It has been established that he has a nuclear weapons program; also, he is widely reputed to be a playboy.

Jenny: Nukes, a real chick magnet.

Koches—Reference to family of Ed Koch, an outspoken former NYC mayor.

Leave It to Beaver—Television comedy that ran from 1957 to 1963 on, first CBS and then ABC, which revolved around the coming of age of young Beaver and his older brother, Wally. The show is best remembered for its idyllic portrayal of suburban American life.

Life with Father—1950s CBS television comedy based on the book and movie of the same name. The show chronicled the lives of a Victorian father, his wife, and their four sons.

Louella Parsons and Hedda Hopper—Powerful arch-rival Hollywood gossip columnists from the late 1930s through the early 1960s.

Love Finds Andy Hardy—1941 romantic comedy featuring Mickey Rooney as Andy Hardy. A popular guy, Hardy gets tangled up with three girls at once, one of whom is played by Judy Garland.

Jenny: Then Mickey went on to get married eight times. None of them to Judy Garland.

Mario Battali—New York City restaurateur, cookbook author, and popular Food Network host who owns eight Italian restaurants in Manhattan.

Jenny: And my favorite Iron Chef. The man is poetry in motion.

Married...with Children—FOX comedy, premiering in 1987 and lasting for eleven seasons, that chronicled the lives of a blue-collar Chicago family, including dim-witted ex-high school football star Al, his big-haired wife, his promiscuous and equally dim-witted daughter, and his very smart but socially awkward son.

Mary Grace Canfield—Actress who played Gomer Pyle's girlfriend in *The Andy Griffith Show*. She was often cast as the "plain" girl, and is best remembered as the clumsy, eccentric carpenter Ralph Monroe in *Green Acres*.

Maureen Dowd asks Are Men Necessary?—Reference to the best-selling book *Are Men Necessary?* by Pulitzer-Prize winning author and columnist Dowd.

Mayberry—Idyllic, bucolic town in which *The Andy Griffith* show was set.

Jenny: Drawls, dust, and fishing holes. It wishes it were Stars Hollow.

Mayflower-descended values—Reference to a rigid, Puritanical mind-set toward morality and socially acceptable behavior.

Meet John Doe—1941 Frank Capra film starring Gary Cooper and Barbara Stanwyk. After the publication of a fraudulent but popular news story, a businessman hires a tramp to be the face of the resulting political movement.

Merry Pranksters—Members of a California commune led by author Ken Kesey, who crisscrossed the United States in a psychedelic bus and held "acid tests" as a way to get people turned on to LSD.

Jenny: Everybody passed.

Meryl Streep—Film, television, and stage star who is considered one of the most talented and respected actresses of her generation. She starred in such films as *Sophie's Choice* and *Kramer vs. Kramer.*

Mickey Rooney and Judy Garland—Duo who starred together in a string of MGM films, including the Andy Hardy series.

Mother Courage and Her Children—Musical adaptation of the play of the same name by Bertolt Brecht, staged by the Public Theater of New York during the 2006 Summer Stage series in Central Park.

Motion Picture Production Code of 1930—Film content guidelines adopted in 1930 and replaced in 1967 by the MPAA rating system. Also known as the Hays Code. The guidelines designated what was morally acceptable in a film in an attempt to save American filmgoers from seeing smut on screen.

Jenny: Thank God it's working.

Mr. Deeds Goes to Town—1936 film directed by Frank Capra and starring Gary Cooper. After a working-class man inherits 20 million dollars, he struggles to avoid the scheming of others.

Mr. Smith Goes to Washington—1939 film directed by Frank Capra and starring Jimmy Stewart. Sent to Washington as a Senate replacement, everyman Jefferson Smith lobbies for a bill to establish a boys' camp. The film won eleven Academy Awards.

Murphy Brown—1988–1998 CBS comedy starring Candice Bergen as a news anchor and journalist. The liberal show tackled such topics as alcoholism and single motherhood.

My Three Sons—Television comedy that ran from 1960 to 1972, first on ABC and then on CBS. The storylines revolved around a single father trying to raise his three sons.

Nancy Reagan—Wife of former president Ronald Reagan and First Lady from 1980–1989, a fashion icon and advocate of the "Just Say No" anti-drug campaign.

Jenny: She has the best inauguration gown in the Smithsonian collection, too.

Newt Gingrich—Conservative Republican who was the speaker of the House of Representatives from 1995 to 1999 and served a total of ten terms in Congress.

Jenny: He also served his first wife divorce papers while she was in the hospital with uterine cancer. What a guy.

Noël Coward—English actor, composer, and playwright who penned both controversial and mainstream plays that attracted large audiences. He was knighted in 1970.

Northern Exposure—1990–1995 CBS series revolving around a young doctor forced to move to quirky small-town Cicely, Alaska, to pay off his student loans.

Nutmeg State—State nickname for Connecticut.

The O.C.—Fox teen-soap hit that premiered in 2003 and followed the lives of outsider Ryan, who was taken in by a family in the O.C., and the other privileged teenagers he met. The show often featured little-known musicians and jumpstarted the careers of featured singers and bands.

Old Faithful—World's most famous geyser. It is located in Yellowstone Park and is characterized by extremely reliable eruptions.

Old North Church—Historic site in Boston built in 1723. It's the church where the "one if by land, two if by sea" lanterns that were a part of Paul Revere's midnight ride were to be hung.

Ozzie and Harriet—Bandleader and his wife who starred in ten-year hit radio show *Ozzie and Harriet* that later became a television series of the same name. The show ran from 1952 to 1966 on ABC and chronicled Ozzie and Harriet's efforts to raise their two sons.

The Patty Duke Show—ABC sitcom about a girl and her identical cousin that ran from 1963 to 1966. The show was created as a star vehicle for Patty Duke.

Paul Revere's house—Tourist attraction located in Boston, Massachusetts. The house was built around 1680 and owned by Revere from 1770 to 1800.

Peyton Place—Steamy, soapy 1957 movie depicting corrupt small-town New England life. The film was based on Grace Metalious's bestselling novel of the same name.

Picket Fences—CBS drama that ran from 1992 to 1996 about the lives of the townspeople of Rome, Wisconsin. The show used bizarre events (such as cows birthing human babies and a murder spree) to deal with politics and ethics.

Playing the Donna Martin to Rory's Kelly Taylor—Reference to popular *Beverly Hills, 90210* characters. Donna Martin was a dedicated virgin with few love interests, while her best friend Kelly Taylor was popular with the boys and prone to bed-hopping.

Jenny: Some things in life are just inexplicable.

Plymouth Rock—Rock where the Pilgrims first disembarked from the Mayflower in 1620.

The prodigal daughter—Reference to Jesus' parable "The Prodigal Son," in which a son squanders his wealth and then returns home to his father, where he is welcomed with open arms and a fatted calf.

Put them all together…and they spell "Father"—Reference to the 1915 Howard Johnson song "M-O-T-H-E-R (A Word That Means the World to Me)."

Roe v. Wade—Controversial landmark 1973 Supreme Court case that ruled that prohibiting abortion violates personal privacy under the Constitution.

"Rumstud"—Media nickname given to Defense Secretary Donald Rumsfeld after Fox News described him as a "babe magnet for the seventy-year-old set."

Jenny: To which the seventy-year-old set replied, "I wouldn't do him with your walker."

Sabrina—1954 film featuring a love triangle between Audrey Hepburn, Humphrey Bogart, and William Holden.

Shirley Booth—Film, radio, and television actress who gained acclaim in such films as *Come Back, Little Sheba* and *A Tree Grows in Brooklyn* but is now primarily remembered for her role as a wisecracking maid in the 1960s television sitcom *Hazel.*

Saturday Evening Post—Weekly magazine published from 1821 to 1969. The publication ran cartoons and articles, but was best known for its fiction.

Saturday Evening Post **covers of Norman Rockwell**—321 covers created by the twentieth-century American artist famous for his idealistic portraits of small-town American life.

Sex and the City—HBO comedy which ran from 1998 to 2004, featuring four friends struggling with love, life, and fashion in Manhattan.

Shakespeare in Central Park—Open-air theater production since 1962, often starring well-known actors.

Smurfy Smurf—Reference to the cartoon show about cheery little blue creatures that live in the forests of Europe, and their often-used adjective, "smurfy."

State House—Boston building built in 1713, the seat of the first elected legislature in America.

Strasbergian Method Acting—Method credited to American acting teacher Lee Strasberg and favored by film stars such as Al Pacino and Robert De Niro.

Steven Seagal—1990s action star best known for his film *Under Siege.*

Sturbridge Village—Large outdoor living history museum that recreates a New England town in the 1830s. It features a country store, a cider mill, a parsonage, and several other businesses and homes.

Sullivan's Travels—Satiric 1941 film written and directed by Preston Sturges and starring Joel McCrea and Veronica Lake about a hotshot young director who sets out to learn about the lives of the poor.

Tab Hunter—1950s and '60s movie star who became a teen idol and ladies' man, and then penned a bestselling autobiography about life as a homosexual in Hollywood.

Taxi Driver—Controversial 1976 Martin Scorsese film starring Robert De Niro as a lonely, deranged taxi driver who practices drawing his gun while shouting "You talking to me?" in a full-length mirror.

Jenny: If he'd been sane, he'd have been practicing his Oscar acceptance speech like the rest of us.

Thelma and Louise—Characters from 1991 movie *Thelma & Louise*, about two women who go on the run after shooting an attempted rapist.

There's Something About Mary—Wildly successful farce starring Ben Stiller and Cameron Diaz.

Thomas Kinkade—Twentieth-century artist often called the "the Painter of Light" who is best known for his mass-production and commercialization of his own work.

Jenny: He makes Hummels look edgy.

Thurston Howell III (*Gilligan's Island*)—Character on *Gilligan's Island* notable for his wealth and social elitism.

Timothy—Companion to the Apostle Paul who had a deep knowledge of scripture. Two books in the New Testament are named after him.

Jenny: And he never let any of the other apostles forget it, either.

Tony the Tiger witness-protection-program style—Reference to the series of television commercials for Frosted Flakes that featured Tony the Tiger seen in "silhouette" to protect his identity.

Trumps—Reference to New York City real estate tycoon Donald Trump and his various wives and offspring.

Veronica Lake—Blonde sex symbol with a peek-a-boo bang who became iconic in the 1940s for her glamour. She starred in such movies as *Sullivan's Travels, I Wanted Wings,* and *I Married a Witch.*

Vidal Sassoon—World-famous hairdresser who developed a popular line of hair care products.

Vivian Vance—Actress best known as Lucy's sidekick Ethel Mertz on the 1950s sitcom *I Love Lucy.*

Wagyu beef burgers—Reference to Chef Daniel Boloud's expensive Kobe beef burger at the New York City restaurant DB Bistro Moderne.

The Wall Street Journal—International daily newspaper that focuses on business and financial news. It was founded in 1889, and has won twenty-nine Pulitzer prizes.

Ward and June Cleaver—Cheery parents of Wally and Beaver on the idyllic 1950s sitcom *Leave It to Beaver.*

Werner Herzog and Klaus Kinski—German film director and actor whose professional relationship was notoriously volatile and sometimes violent.

Wicked Witch of the West—Character from the beloved children's book and movie *The Wizard of Oz.* The term is usually a reference to someone evil.

Jenny: But she had great shoes.

William Holden—Hollywood actor who starred in *Stalag 17* and *Sunset Boulevard.* J. D. Salinger saw his name on a marquee and used it for his protagonist in *Catcher in the Rye.*

Acknowledgments

Thanks to Erica Lovett for her work on "*Coffee At Luke's*-isms." Thanks also to Nicole Robillard of GilmoreFan.com for her assistance reviewing the manuscript.

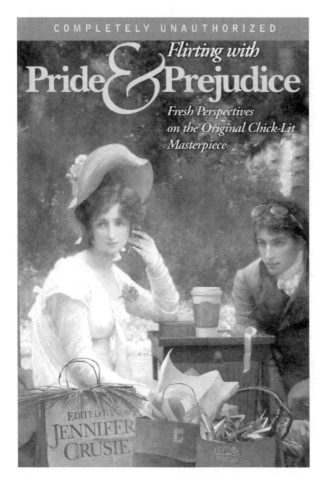

Jane Austen's *Pride and Prejudice* is one of the most beloved novels of our time, transcending the literary world to earn a spot on every woman's nightstand. Now, *Flirting with Pride and Prejudice* takes a fresh and humorous look at Austen's classic tale of looking for Mr. Right, marrying rich and finding true love in the process.

benbellabooks.com

More than just a high school drama, *Veronica Mars* is a smart and savvy teen detective show that offers complex mysteries and rapier wit, engaging social commentary, and noir sensibilities—with the occasional murder thrown in for good measure. This collection, edited by the creator and executive producer of the show, offers supreme insight into the class struggles and love stories of the series.

smartpopbooks.com

Speculating about the cultural metaphors in Janet Evanovich's wildly popular mystery series (which includes 11 books), this anthology takes a look at lingerie-buyer-turned-bounty-hunter Stephanie Plum and catalogs her bad luck with cars (she's blown up quite a few), her good luck with men, her unorthodox approach to weapon storage, and the rich tapestry of her milieu: Trenton, New Jersey, also known as The Burg.

benbellabooks.com

4/17 Worped top corner   CS

BOCA RATON PUBLIC LIBRARY, FLORIDA

3 3656 0374672 6

IF YOU LIKE C

COMPLETELY UNAUTHORIZED

GREY'S ANATOMY 101

791.4572 Cof

Coffee at Luke's

JUN   2007

SEATTLE GRACE, UNAUTHORIZED
Edited by Leah Wilson

The 2005-2006 season's smash hit *Grey's Anatomy* swiftly eclipsed its *Desperate Housewives* lead-in, in ratings, in critical claim, and in vocal viewer enthusiasm. What could have been just another hospital drama is elevated by sharp, clever writing, strong female characters, and a stellar ensemble cast of multi-ethnic actors. With 20+ million viewers tuning in every week, *Grey's Anatomy* was the new must-see television show of the year. From lighthearted relationship speculations to analyses of deeper themes, *Grey's Anatomy 101* gives new perspectives on all facets of the series.

smartpopbooks.com